The Latest Wok
Cookbook for Beginners

Essential Wok Recipes for Beginners | incl. Simple, Varied, and Delicious Dishes to Fuel Healthy Eating

Tiffany Tunnell

CONTENTS

Introduction

If you enjoy cooking Chinese dishes, investing in a good wok will be worth it. A wok is an excellent solution to kitchen dilemmas. Use this kitchen marvel to whip up quick and flavor-packed stir-fries that add excitement to your dining experience.

The true beauty of Chinese food lies in its simplicity. Just by selecting a few ingredients and the right flavorful spices, anybody can create the most impressive and delicious Chinese dishes in no time. Chinese Cuisine developed from different areas of China and soon became very popular worldwide for its unique cooking style and flavor. There are eight central cuisines in China. Chinese foods are mainly comprised of two components, that are grains and meat. Starch and vegetables are essential ingredients of all dishes. The necessary foundation of most Chinese dishes is garlic, ginger, and sesame. Soy sauce is used in all cuisines for saltiness. Stir-frying is an essential technique to cook Chinese Cuisines. A wok is used to stir-fry vegetables in garlic.

Chinese Cuisine got popular when Chinese immigrants came to America and worked in food shops. Many traditional Chinese dishes gained popularity in America. Thus, many chefs in the United States changed Chinese cooking style; hence Chinese-American dishes emerged. Chinese Cuisine is not only tasty, but also healthy and nutritious. Spices used in Chinese cooking are full of nutrients that a human body needs to work the whole day. These are rich sources of carbohydrates, starch, proteins, and fibers.

This Chinese wok cookbook is a collection of the best recipes, using simple, readily available ingredients and various cooking methods. Although the recipes are different, they have some things in common: Nutritious and easy to prepare, even for beginners. Preparing self-cooked meals is only a challenge at first, but you will soon discover that it is both rewarding and fulfilling. The best part is that you do not have to be a professional chef or have every single Asian ingredient at your disposal to put together these dishes. All you need is the right ingredients, the right tools, and the strong desire to make these dishes to make it possible.

So, let's not waste any more time.

Let's get right into it!

Brief History of Wok

The ultimate kitchen implement, this 2,000-year-old magical cooking pot, is a way of life all over Asia. Perfect for sautéing, braising, frying, and steaming, it can be a lifesaver on busy days. The word wok simply means pan in Cantonese. In the Mandarin dialect, a wok is referred to as a Kuo. Woks were developed around 2,000 years ago and are still the ideal vessels for stir-frying today. The wok's small, rounded bottom makes efficient use of limited fuel by concentrating heat and then distributing it evenly along the curved surface, eliminating hot spots that may cause food to stick and burn. The curve also allows the oil and ingredients to move to the wok's hottest part. This creates the stir-fry's signature high sizzle, quickly searing in flavor and juice and imparting a subtle smoky flavor known as wok hei, which metaphorically translates to breath of the wok.

Woks are traditionally made by hammering a carbon steel disk into a bowl shape and attaching one or two handles. Wok-like pans are used throughout Asia and different cultures have customized the versatile pan to fit their needs. For example, the Cantonese wok, also known as a two-eared wok, has two small, curved handles on each side. A Northern-style wok usually has one long removable wooden handle, sometimes with a handle on the opposite side for lifting when the wok is full. The Japanese refer to their wok-shaped pans as Chukanabe, while in Southern India, their wok-shaped pans are called Cheena Chatti. Both translate roughly to Chinese pot. Nowadays, woks come in many different shapes, sizes, and materials. When it comes to shape, woks are typically either round-bottomed or flat-bottomed. Round-bottomed woks were designed to be used over an open flame, so they are best suited for a gas stove-top. If you have a round-bottomed wok but an electric stove, place the wok ring that comes with the pan with the broader edge facing up to cradle the wok closest to the heat source. It might take a little more time for the wok to heat up since the heat is indirect, but the electric burner should maintain adequate stir-frying temperature once hot.

In contrast, flat-bottomed woks were developed to accommodate flat-topped electric burners. If using a flat-bottomed wok, you may need to use a little more

oil to compensate for hot spots that naturally occur. Hot spots are parts of the pan where the seasoning begins to burn; swirl the oil over those areas before adding any ingredients to prevent the food from burning.

The Chinese Kitchen

Chinese Cuisine involves more than forty distinct ways to cook foods, making them rich in taste and aroma. The following are the most prominent Chinese cooking methods.

炒 (Chǎo)

Stir-frying is one of the most common cooking methods. Raw ingredients are cut into small pieces, they are added to a heated oil pot. Furthermore, salt, spices, and MSG are added according to the recipe. Afterward, starch is added to bind the stir-fried veggies to the sauce in the pot before serving.

炝 (Qiàng)

Ingredients are sliced first and then put into boiling water for a relatively short time. Afterward, spices are added after thoroughly draining the water.

煮 (Zhǔ)

This method involves boiling food in a mixture of spices and water. 煎 (Jiān) This method involves putting the ingredients in a pot with some oil and heating it until the food becomes golden-brown.

炸 (Zhá)

It is considered one of the famous, notable, and convenient cooking methods involving heating half a pot of oil to higher temperatures and cooking the food in hot oil. Mainly spices are added before frying the food.

涮 (Shuàn)

Initially, the food is sliced thoroughly, put into boiling water, then dipped into a sauce to eat. The famous hot pot dish is usually prepared with this cooking method.

There are different branches of Chinese Cuisine, including Lu Cuisine, Su Cuisine, Zhe Cuisine, Xiang Cuisine, Hui Cuisine, Chuan Cuisine, Yue Cuisine, and Min Cuisine. These eight branches of Chinese Cuisine primarily focus on nutritious foods and giving an artistic touch to foods.

Basics of Wok

There are many different types of woks, and it's essential to know the pros and cons of each so you know what you're working with and can make the most of the wok you have.

Carbon-Steel Woks

Carbon-steel woks are the woks used in restaurants and many Chinese homes. Made from cold-forged carbon-steel, they are incredibly durable if properly cared for, and they are also the most inexpensive woks on the market. Carbon-steel is an excellent heat conductor and is ideal for achieving wok hei. Like cast-iron woks, carbon-steel woks must be washed by hand, dried over heat, and oiled after each use to keep them from rusting. A well-seasoned carbon-steel wok develops a black patina over time and becomes essentially nonstick. For stir-frying and deep-frying, we find the carbon-steel wok to be the best type of wok. If your budget allows, we suggest having another wok or pan designated for steaming and braising because the moisture can ruin the patina you've worked so hard to build up in your carbon-steel wok.

Cast-Iron Woks

A Chinese cast-iron wok is thinner and lighter than American and European cast-iron pans but still heavier than carbon-steel woks. Chinese cast-iron woks are

usually found in Chinese or Asian specialty stores and can be used over gas, electric, or induction stove-tops. Cast-iron woks are great for deep-frying and steaming because they are heavier than carbon-steel woks and retain more extended heat. However, like carbon-steel woks, they require extra work to maintain their seasoning and to prevent rusting.

Stainless-Steel Woks

Stainless-steel woks are also great conductors of heat, and they require no seasoning or special maintenance. All you need to do is thoroughly clean them with soap and water as you would any other stainless-steel pan to avoid buildup. These woks are perfect for braising and steaming in addition to stir-frying, because you don't have to worry about rust and water damage. However, you may find that you need a little more cooking oil when using a stainless-steel wok. Stainless- steel woks can be used over gas, electric, or induction stove-tops.

Non-Stick Woks

Non-stick woks are the new kids on the block. Their advantages are that they don't rust or need to be seasoned. They are great for cooks who use their woks infrequently because they are easy to clean and don't require constant maintenance. However non-stick woks can be pricey. Because wok cooking is all about high heat, we recommend only high-quality non-Teflon/non-coated non-stick woks meant to be used over high heat. Wok hei cannot be fully achieved with a non-stick wok, but if your goal is to reduce the amount of oil used in stir-frying, this wok is for you. Be sure to use wooden or silicone utensils so as not to damage the non-stick surface. Most non-stick woks can be used over gas, electric, or induction stove-tops (check manufacturer's recommendations to be sure).

Electric Woks

You can't beat an electric wok for portability and versatility. The major drawback to using an electric wok for stir-frying is, it doesn't get hot enough. Electric woks are usually nonstick, so they are as easy to clean as any other nonstick pan. Make sure to use wooden or silicone utensils, so you don't scratch the wok interior. Electric woks cannot be immersed in water, so be careful not to get the electrical components wet.

Shape and size matter carbon-steel and cast-iron woks are available in both flat- and round-bottomed versions, whereas nonstick and stainless-steel woks are typically only flat-bottomed. Flat-bottomed woks can rest on the stovetop without tipping over. Round-bottomed woks need a wok ring to keep them stable. Flat-bottomed woks allow for more even heating than round-bottomed woks. Round-bottomed woks are used exclusively over a gas burner. A flat-bottomed wok is suitable for electric and gas stovetops; it is also the only wok that works with induction stove-tops.

Using Tips for Wok

Ingredient Prep: Prepare and measure everything before you start cooking. Slice and marinate your proteins, cut your veggies, and mix up your sauces before you even turn on the stove. Line them up next to the stove in the order they will be cooked. Wok cooking is fast! You won't have time for prepping once you start cooking, so do it all before turning on the heat.

Heating:

1. Get the wok hot.
2. For stir-frying, heat your wok over medium-high heat - until a drop of water sizzles and evaporates on contact if there's no sizzle, your wok is not hot enough.
3. Make sure your wok is completely dry before moving on to the next step.

Oil: Use a high-smoke-point oil. For stir-frying, it's essential to use an oil that will not burn at high temperatures, like vegetable, grapeseed, and avocado. Steer clear of extra-virgin olive oil, which will burn and smoke over high heat. Sesame oil should be added only at the end because it will burn if used at the beginning when your wok is at its hottest. Pour in the oil, then swirl it around to coat the bottom of the wok.

Seasoning the Oil. Season the oil by adding the aromatics - ginger and a pinch of salt first, then garlic if you're using it. Seasoning the oil leads to balanced, nuanced flavors and is a must in our book. Pay close attention so you don't burn the aromatics.

Spatula: Use your wok spatula to scoop, toss, and flip what you are cooking.

Cook Ingredients in the Proper Order: Cook the protein first and transfer it to a bowl. Then cook the vegetables, adding the hardest to the wok first and the

softest last. Hard and dense vegetables take longer to cook than soft, delicate vegetables. Once all the vegetables are crisp, return the protein to the pan and add the sauce.

Sauces: Add the sauce around the outside edge of the pan. This technique helps prevent heat loss from the wok. As you add the sauce, toss the ingredients in it.

Wok Crowding: Don't overload your wok. When you fill a wok to the brim, your ingredients will steam rather than stir-fry.

Caring for your Wok

To keep your wok in good condition and ready for use, below are essential tips:

• When cooking, always heat the wok until it's hot before adding oil.

• **Cleaning:** Never wash your seasoned wok with soap. Rinse it with warm water, and wipe it with a gentle sponge or brush. Don't abrasively scrub your wok, as that will affect the seasoning layer. Don't use steel pads or scouring sponges on the inside, though you can use them on the outside of your wok if it gets dirty.

• **Drying:** For a new wok, you might want to dry it over high heat after you rinse it. For a well-seasoned wok, wipe until dry. Don't let it sit around wet, it could develop rust if that happens.

• **Seasoning:** New woks need oil to continue developing their seasoning layer. So don't do a lot of poaching with a newly seasoned wok - do a lot of stir-frying! Over time, your wok will become deeper in color, and the seasoning layer will develop. Once this happens, you can wipe out your wok with a paper towel like a nonstick pan. The more you cook with your wok, the better seasoned it will be. If you don't use your wok often, rub a small amount of peanut oil onto the inside surface of the wok before storing it. If you forget about your wok for a while and it gets rusty or if it gets very burned once you use it again, then do a full re-seasoning of it.

How to Season your Wok:

Your wok will come home from the store smelling like oil. This oil is a preservative applied by the manufacturer. It will need to be cleaned off the wok.

Step 1. Wash the wok in soapy water, and scrub it clean on the inside and the outside.

Step 2. Now you need to burn the wok. Place it on the stove, and dry it over very high heat.

Step 3. Remove the wok from the heat, and put a few tablespoons of peanut oil on the bottom of the wok. Using a dry cloth, spread a thin layer of the oil entirely over the inside surface of the wok. Be careful not to burn yourself.

Step 4. Over very high heat, heat the oil in the wok for a few minutes. Turn off the heat, take the wok off it, and let it cool to room temperature.

Step 5. Once the wok is at room temperature, put it on high heat again, ensuring the first layer of oil gets burned into the wok. Turn off the heat, take the pan off the stove, and return the pan to room temperature again.

Step 6. Once at room temperature, add another thin layer of oil, and spread it over the inside surface of the wok, as you did in step 3.

Step 7. Heat the wok again for a few minutes, and then turn off the heat, take the pan off the heat, and return it to room temperature once more.

Step 8. Repeat steps 5 and 6 a few more times.

Step 9. Wipe off any excess oil that collects in the bottom center of the wok. Once the wok starts to darken and look shiny, it's ready to use.

The more you cook with your wok, the better its seasoning will be and the less oil you'll have to use when cooking with it. Re-season your wok if it becomes necessary.

4-Week Meal Plan

Week 1

Day 1:
Breakfast: Nutritious Steamed Egg Scallion Custard
Lunch: Refreshing Sweet-Sour Veggies
Snack: Yummy Buttered Egg Puffs
Dinner: Nutritious Chicken and Green Beans
Dessert: Quick Stir-Fried Bananas Foster

Day 2:
Breakfast: Egg Pork Dumplings
Lunch: Easy Sesame Shiitake Stir-fry
Snack: Spicy Cold Seaweed Salad
Dinner: Simple Beef Stir-fry with Broccoli
Dessert: Stir-Fried Spiced Apples Shortcake

Day 3:
Breakfast: Homemade Fried Eggs with Peas
Lunch: Delicious Vegetables and Tofu in a Peanut Sauce
Snack: Golden Brown Banana Fritters
Dinner: Easy Fish in Oyster Sauce
Dessert: Sweet Sesame Balls

Day 4:
Breakfast: Fried Carrot and Pork Wontons
Lunch: Homemade Tso Tofu
Snack: Savory Wok-Fried Salty Peanuts
Dinner: Classic Kung Pao Chicken
Dessert: Homemade Peach Squares

Day 5:
Breakfast: Delicious Siri Lankan Spicy Breakfast Omelet
Lunch: Garlic Lettuce Stir-fry
Snack: Sesame Rice Ball
Dinner: Savory Beef Chow Fun
Dessert: Snow Fungus Soup with Pears and Dates

Day 6:
Breakfast: Buttered Banana Breakfast
Lunch: Garlic Bitter Melon with Red Wine Vinegar
Snack: Coconut Rice Pudding with Nuts
Dinner: Chinese Clams in Black Bean Sauce
Dessert: Refreshing Lime Parsley Calamari

Day 7:
Breakfast: Homemade Delicious Shashuka
Lunch: Sesame Tofu and Mushroom
Snack: Quick Egg Noodles
Dinner: Refreshing Pork Stir Fry Pineapple and Peppers
Dessert: Milky Mango Sago

Week 2

Day 1:
Breakfast: Traditional Breakfast Poha
Lunch: Southwest Tofu Scramble
Snack: Sweet Coconut Corn Pudding
Dinner: Garlic Chicken and Vegetables
Dessert: Tasty Snow Skin Mooncakes

Day 2:
Breakfast: Meat Breakfast Hash
Lunch: Spicy Garlic Szechuan Eggplant
Snack: Easy Spicy Bamboo Shoot Salad
Dinner: Delicious Steak and Brussels Sprouts
Dessert: Golden Almond Syrup

Day 3:
Breakfast: Breakfast Fried Egg and Tomatoes
Lunch: Healthy Cabbage Burji and Carrots
Snack: Easy Steamed Milk Custard
Dinner: Nutritious Shrimp with Grains & Egg
Dessert: Yummy Sweet Rice Balls with Black Sesame

Day 4:
Breakfast: Nutritious Scrambled Egg with Salmon
Lunch: Spicy Okra Stir-fry
Snack: Wok-Fried Vanilla Pears
Dinner: Classic Mongolian Chicken
Dessert: Easy Millet Congee

Day 5:
Breakfast: Cinnamon Red Bean Bun
Lunch: Homemade Ginger Sesame Tofu
Snack: Stir-Fried Sweet Crullers
Dinner: Celery Beef with Tomatoes
Dessert: Butter Osmanthus Cake

Day 6:
Breakfast: Tasty Dandelion Pork Dumplings
Lunch: Garlic Zucchini Broccoli Stir Fry
Snack: Homemade Coconut Banana Fritters
Dinner: Fried Garlic Fish Fillets
Dessert: Classic Chinese Sweet Peanut Cream Dessert

Day 7:
Breakfast: Classic Chinese Eggs Stewed in Tea
Lunch: Tasty Almond and Vegetable Stir-Fry
Snack: Lime-Marinated Calamari with Italian Parsley
Dinner: Traditional Pork Adobo
Dessert: Traditional Sichuan Chicken and Vegetables

Week 3

Day 1:
Breakfast: Yummy Crispy Omelet
Lunch: Healthy Teriyaki Burgers
Snack: Sticky Coconut and Peanut Mochi
Dinner: Sesame Basil Chicken with Bell Peppers
Dessert: Delicious Steamed White Sugar Sponge Cake

Day 2:
Breakfast: Sweet Egg Tarts
Lunch: Japanese Style Spring Stir Fry
Snack: Fried Cream Wontons with Scallions
Dinner: Onion Beef Lo Mein
Dessert: Authentic Chinese Chili Chicken Dry

Day 3:
Breakfast: Healthy Vegetable Dumplings
Lunch: Garlic Cabbage Scrambled with Chicken Dice
Snack: Easy Fried Sweet Bananas
Dinner: Healthy Scrambled Broccoli with Shrimp
Dessert: Healthy Sugar and Vinegar with Cucumber Salad

Day 4:
Breakfast: Sweet Coconut Bun
Lunch: Homemade Apple Ramen Salad
Snack: Homemade Eggy Scallion Dumplings
Dinner: Classic Sweet and Sour Chicken
Dessert: Tamari Mongolian Chicken

Day 5:
Breakfast: Tasty Bacon and Egg Fried Rice
Lunch: Japanese Flavorful Dashi Omelet
Snack: Caramel Cinnamon Caramel Granola
Dinner: Yummy Spicy Beef and Eggplant
Dessert: Delicious Cornstarch with Berries and Pork Balls

Day 6:
Breakfast: Veggie and Pork Rolls
Lunch: Sweet and Spicy Ramen Stir Fry with Spinach
Snack: Delicious Spiced Popcorn
Dinner: Lemony Trout Fillets with Onions
Dessert: Peppered Sesame Edamame

Day 7:
Breakfast: Marinated Shrimp Dumplings with Bamboo Shoots
Lunch: Delicious Sweet Ramen with Tofu
Snack: Chinese Sesame Steamed Egg Custard
Dinner: Classic Xi'an Lamb Burgers
Dessert: Crispy Fried Shrimp Balls

Week 4

Day 1:
Breakfast: Garlic Carrot Mushroom Dumplings with Sauce
Lunch: Sesame Broccoli with Soy-Oyster Sauce
Snack: Simple Egg Foo Young with Gravy
Dinner: Chinese Chicken and Tofu Clash Stir Fry
Dessert: Simple Apple Cinnamon Coffee Cake

Day 2:
Breakfast: Homemade Delicious Shashuka
Lunch: Simple Daikon Radish
Snack: Fresh Milky Mango Pudding
Dinner: Traditional Mongolian Beef and Broccoli
Dessert: Ketchup Cucumber with Koya Dofu

Day 3:
Breakfast: Classic Chinese Tea Eggs
Lunch: Yummy Sichuan Eggplant in Sauce
Snack: Homemade Steamed Scallion Buns
Dinner: Tasty Scrambled Shrimp with Eggplant
Dessert: Crispy Oniony Coconut Shrimp

Day 4:
Breakfast: Meat Breakfast Hash
Lunch: Savory Garlic Almond Bean Stir-Fry
Snack: Crispy Buttered Egg Puffs
Dinner: Mayo Honey Chicken Stir Fry
Dessert: Healthy Chili Cilantro and Seaweed Salad

Day 5:
Breakfast: Nutritious Scrambled Egg with Salmon
Lunch: Healthy Veggie Bowl
Snack: Chinese Tea-Soaked Eggs
Dinner: Ginger Beef Ramen with Vegetables
Dessert: Yummy Milky Coconut and Peanut Mochi

Day 6:
Breakfast: Veggie and Tofu Dumplings
Lunch: Salty Garlic Asparagus Stir-Fry
Snack: Golden Brown Banana Fritters
Dinner: Tasty Halibut Fillets in Tau Cheo Sauce
Dessert: Homemade Fried Sesame with Sugar Balls

Day 7:
Breakfast: Nutritious Steamed Egg Scallion Custard
Lunch: Bok Choy and Broccoli Stir Fry in Oyster Sauce
Snack: Sweet Creamy Almond Sponge Cake
Dinner: Crispy Pork Schnitzel
Dessert: Spicy Pork and Cabbage Potstickers

Chapter 1 Breakfast

Chive Pork Dumplings with Chili Sauce

Prep Time: 15 minutes | Cook Time: 60 minutes | Serves: 5

½ cup soy sauce
1 tablespoon seasoned rice vinegar
1 tablespoon Chinese chives, finely chopped
1 tablespoon sesame seeds
1 teaspoon chili-garlic sauce
1 pound ground pork
3 cloves garlic, minced
1 egg, beaten
2 tablespoons Chinese chives, finely chopped
2 tablespoons soy sauce
1 ½ tablespoon sesame oil
1 tablespoon fresh ginger, minced
50 dumpling wrappers
1 cup vegetable oil, for frying
1-quart water, or more as needed

1. Combine ½ cup of soy sauce, rice vinegar, sesame seeds, 1 tablespoon chives, and chili sauce in a small bowl. 2. Combine the pork, garlic, sesame oil, 2 tablespoons of chives, egg, soy sauce, and ginger in a large mixing bowl. 3. Place 1 spoonful of the filling in the center of a dumpling wrapper on a lightly floured work surface. To seal the dumpling, wet the edge with a little water and pinch it together to produce little pleats. Continue with the remaining dumpling wrappers and filling. 4. Heat 1 to 2 tablespoons vegetable oil over medium-high heat in a large pan. Cook until browned, about 2 minutes per side, with 8 to 10 dumplings in the pan. Pour in 1 cup of water, cover, and cook for 5 minutes until cooked. 5. Continue with the remaining dumplings. 6. When cooking is finished, serve.

Delicious Stir-Fried Egg and Tomato

Prep Time: 5 minutes | Cook Time: 5 minutes | Serves: 4

4 eggs
2 tablespoons Shaoxing wine
1 teaspoon chicken stock granules
1½ teaspoons salt
1 dash ground white pepper
4 tablespoons cooking oil
2 medium tomatoes
1½ teaspoons sugar
2 stalks scallions

1. Whisk together the eggs, Shaoxing wine, chicken stock granules, salt, and powdered white Pepper in a mixing bowl. Beat the eggs until slightly foamy. 2. Heat 3 tablespoons of cooking oil over medium-high heat in a wok. Before scrambling the eggs, pour the egg mixture into the wok and leave it alone for about 20 seconds. 3. While the scrambled eggs are still soft and runny, remove them from the wok. Toss the tomato wedges in the wok with 1 tablespoon of frying oil. 4. Allow the tomatoes to burn for around 30 seconds before flipping them. 5. Return the eggs to the wok once the tomatoes have softened. To blend, stir everything together. 6. Sprinkle the sugar over the eggs and tomatoes and whisk to spread it around the dish thoroughly. 7. Remove the pan from the heat and place in the scallions. Place on a serving platter. 8. Serve.

Chinese Chives Egg Stir-Fry

Prep Time: 10 minutes | Cook Time: 5 minutes | Serves: 2

5 large eggs
⅛ teaspoon sugar
½ teaspoon salt
1 teaspoon Shaoxing wine
¼ teaspoon ground white pepper
¼ teaspoon sesame oil
4 teaspoons water
2 cups Chinese chives/garlic chives, chopped
4 tablespoons vegetable oil

1. Crack the eggs and whisk in the sugar, salt, white pepper, Shaoxing wine, sesame oil, and water in a large mixing bowl. For a good 30 seconds, beat the eggs until you see a layer of little bubbles floating on top of the beaten eggs. 2. Mix in the chives until they're evenly distributed. You are now ready to cook. 3. Heat the wok until it just begins to smoke, then reduce to medium-low heat. After 10 seconds, drizzle in the oil. 4. Using your spatula, swirl the oil around in the wok. The oil should be heated but not smoked when adding the egg mixture. 5. After pouring the eggs into the pan, softly flip and toss them with a spatula, careful not to brown or harden up the eggs too much. They're done when the eggs are just cooked. Serve!

Egg Pork Dumplings

Prep Time: 35 minutes | Cook Time: 30 minutes | Serves: 5

4 eggs
2 teaspoons cornstarch
1 teaspoon water
¼ teaspoon salt
3 ounces ground pork
3 water chestnuts, minced
1½ teaspoons green onions, finely chopped
1 teaspoon cornstarch
½ teaspoon fresh ginger, finely shredded
½ teaspoon white sugar
½ teaspoon salt
¼ teaspoon toasted sesame oil
¾ cup chicken broth
1 tablespoon soy sauce
½ teaspoon dry sherry
¼ teaspoon salt
½ teaspoon white sugar
¼ teaspoon black pepper

1. Whisk the eggs, 2 tablespoons cornstarch, water, and ¼ teaspoon salt in a mixing bowl. Set aside for 25 minutes. 2. In a mixing bowl, combine the pork, water chestnuts, green onions, 1 teaspoon cornstarch, ginger, ½ teaspoon of sugar, ½ teaspoon of salt, and toasted sesame oil, kneading thoroughly. 3. Cover the bowl with plastic wrap and keep it in the refrigerator until you're ready to use it. 4. Spray a non-stick wok with cooking spray and heat over medium heat. One tablespoon of the egg mixture should be slowly poured into the wok. (This will make one egg wrapper.) 5. Allow the egg to cook for 1 minute or until firm on the bottom but still moist on top. Continue in the same way with the rest of the egg mixture. As you finish the egg wrappers, stack them on a wax-paper-lined platter and set them aside to cool. 6. In a saucepan, combine the soy sauce, chicken broth, sherry, ¼ teaspoon of salt, ½ teaspoon of sugar, and black pepper, and bring to a moderate simmer. 7. Place about 1 teaspoon of pork filling in the center of each wrapper, fold over to produce a half-moon shape, and gently press to seal. 8. Drop the filled dumplings into the seasoned chicken stock and cook for 10 to 15 minutes until the filling is cooked through. 9. When cooking is finished, serve.

Nutritious Steamed Egg Scallion Custard

Prep Time: 10 minutes | Cook Time: 10 minutes | Serves: 4

4 large eggs, at room temperature
1¾ cups low-sodium chicken broth or filtered water
2 teaspoons Shaoxing rice wine
½ teaspoon Kosher salt
2 scallions, green part only, thinly sliced
4 teaspoons sesame oil

1. In a large bowl, whisk the eggs. Add the broth and rice wine and whisk to combine. 2. Strain the egg mixture through a fine-mesh sieve set over a liquid measuring cup to remove air bubbles. 3. Pour the egg mixture into 4 (6 ounces) ramekins. With a paring knife, pop any bubbles on the surface of the egg mixture. 4. Cover the ramekins with aluminum foil. 5. Rinse a bamboo steamer basket and its lid under cold water and place it in the wok. 6. Pour in 2 inches of water, or until it comes above the bottom rim of the steamer by ¼ to ½ inch, but not so much that it touches the bottom of the basket. 7. Place the ramekins in the steamer basket. Cover with the lid. 8. Bring the water to a boil and reduce the heat to a low simmer. Steam over low heat for about 10 minutes or until the eggs are just set. 9. Carefully remove the ramekins from the steamer and serve immediately.

Yummy Stir Fry Herb Omelet

Prep Time: 10 minutes | Cook Time: 5 minutes | Serves: 2

3 free-range eggs, medium
1 tablespoon of butter (unsalted)
1 tablespoon chopped flat-leaf parsley
1 tablespoon chopped chives
Salt and pepper to taste

1. In a mixing dish, crack the eggs and whisk spices and eggs together until thoroughly blended with the yolks and whites. 2. Preheat a wok. Add the butter once the wok is heated. Pour in the egg mixture. 3. Stir gently for 15-20 seconds using a spatula. Reduce the heat to low and sprinkle the parsley and chives around the omelet's center. 4. Fold a third of the omelet towards the center of the pan as soon as the egg starts to set on the bottom. 5. Remove the omelet and serve.

Tasty Dandelion Pork Dumplings

Prep Time: 70 minutes | Cook Time: 50 minutes | Serves: 10

2 pounds ground pork
2 cups dandelion greens, minced
3 cups napa cabbage, minced
½ cup bok choy leaves, minced
4 green onions, white and light green parts only, minced
1 tablespoon fresh ginger root, chopped
3 cloves garlic, minced
1 (8-ounce) can bamboo shoots, drained and minced
3 tablespoons soy sauce
1 teaspoon white pepper
1 teaspoon kosher salt
1 teaspoon white sugar
4 teaspoons sesame oil
1 egg whites
1 tablespoon water
100 wonton wrappers
½ cup vegetable oil
2 teaspoons chili oil, or to taste

1. Mix 4 teaspoons of sesame oil, pork, dandelion greens, napa cabbage, bok choy, 4 chopped green onions, 1 tablespoon ginger, 3 garlic cloves, bamboo shoots, 3 tablespoons soy sauce, white pepper, salt, 1 teaspoon sugar, and 3 tablespoons soy sauce. Place in the refrigerator to chill for 6 to 8 hours or overnight. 2. Whisk the egg white with the water and leave it aside in a separate dish. Working one at a time, spoon 1 tablespoon of the pork mixture into a wonton wrapper. 3. Cover the additional wrappers with a damp cloth to keep them from drying out. Brush the egg white mixture along the edges of the wrapper. Fold the wrapper in half and seal the edges with a moistened fork. 4. Use cooking spray to coat a big wok. Heat 2 teaspoons of vegetable oil over medium-high heat. Place the dumplings, seam side up, onto the wok in batches. Cook for 30 seconds to 1 minute until the dumplings color slightly. 5. Cover the wok with half a cup of water. Steam the dumplings for 7 to 8 minutes or until the oil and water begin to crackle. 6. Once the water has evaporated, flip the dumplings and cook for another 3 to 5 minutes, or until the bottoms begin to brown. Repeat with the remaining dumplings, oil, and water in batches. 7. When cooking is finished, serve.

Fried Carrot and Pork Wontons

Prep Time: 10 minutes | Cook Time: 0 minutes | Serves: 4

1 pound ground pork
2 garlic cloves, minced
1 teaspoon minced fresh ginger
1 teaspoon toasted sesame oil
1 tablespoon soy sauce
5 scallions, finely chopped
2 carrots, finely chopped
40 wonton wrappers
Peanut oil, for deep-frying

1. Mix the pork, garlic, ginger, soy sauce, scallions, sesame oil and carrots in a large bowl. 2. In the center of a wonton wrapper, place about a teaspoon of the pork filling. 3. Dampen the edges of the wonton wrapper with a bit of water, and fold the edges over to make a triangle. 4. Using your fingers, press the edges together to seal the wonton. 5. To a wok, add enough of the peanut oil so that it is about 1½ inches deep. Heat the oil to 350° F. 6. Fry 5 or 6 wontons at a time until they're golden brown. Continue until all are fried. 7. Drain the finished wontons on a rack or a plate covered with paper towels.

Homemade Delicious Shashuka

Prep Time: 30 minutes | Cook Time: 15 minutes | Serves: 3

Chopped fresh chives, as required
Eggs, twelve
Onion, one
Chopped garlic, one teaspoon
Butter, two tablespoon
Chopper tomatoes, half cup
Salt, to taste
Black pepper, to taste

1. In a large wok, add the butter and let it melt down. 2. Add in the chopped onion. 3. Cook the onion until soft. 4. Add in the garlic. 5. Mix the onions and garlic for two minutes and add in the tomatoes. 6. Add the eggs and do not mix. 7. Add in the salt and pepper. 8. Cover the wok. 9. When the eggs are done, dish them out. 10. Add the fresh chopped chives on top. 11. Your dish is ready to be served.

Classic Chinese Eggs Stewed in Tea

Prep Time: 10 minutes | Cook Time: 15 minutes | Serves: 12

12 eggs
2 slices ginger
3-star anise
1 cinnamon stick
2 bay leaves
2 tablespoons black tea leaves
1 teaspoon Sichuan peppercorns
3 tablespoons light soy sauce
4 teaspoons dark soy sauce
1 teaspoon sugar
2 teaspoons salt
2 tablespoons Shaoxing wine
7 cups water

1. Allow the eggs to get to room temperature by taking them out of the fridge for a few hours. 2. Meanwhile, make the sauce base by combining the remaining ingredients in a medium pot. Bring the mixture to a boil, then reduce the heat to low and keep it there. Cook for 10 minutes with the lid on, then remove it from the heat, open the top, and leave it aside to cool entirely. 3. For the eggs, bring a pot of water to a boil. Gently and swiftly lower the eggs into the boiling water using a big spoon. Allow 7 minutes for the eggs to cook in boiling water. Turn off the heat and transfer to an ice bath after the timer goes off. Allow to chill in the ice bath for as long as possible. 4. Lightly crack the eggshells once the eggs have cooled. Here, the idea is to create enough cracks for the sauce base flavor to penetrate the egg. 5. Soak the broken eggs in the sauce base in the refrigerator for 24 hours, ensuring that all eggs are completely soaked. They're ready in 24 hours! You can even soak them for a longer period if you want a stronger flavor. In the refrigerator, these eggs will last 3 to 4 days.

Tasty Scrambled Egg with Shrimps

Prep Time: 10 minutes | Cook Time: 25 minutes | Serves: 2

4 ounces peeled and deveined shrimp
4 big eggs
¼ cup of chicken broth or stock
Salt and pepper to taste
½ teaspoon rice wine from China
1 teaspoon sauce (oyster)
1 finely sliced green onion
2 tablespoons oil

1. Wash the shrimp well and wipe dry with the paper towels. Make a reservation. 2. Lightly whisk the eggs in a medium mixing basin. 3. Chicken broth, salt, rice wine, pepper, oyster sauce, and green onion should be added to the eggs. Stir until everything is thoroughly combined. 4. Preheat a wok or a large pan over medium-high heat. In a hot wok, pour one tablespoon of oil. 5. Add the shrimp when the oil is extremely hot. 6. Stir-fry the shrimp briefly until they become pink. Remove it from the wok. 7. Turn the heat to high and add the remaining tablespoon of oil to the wok. Add the egg mixture when the oil is extremely hot. 8. Scramble for approximately 1 minute before adding the shrimp. 9. Serve.

Veggie and Tofu Dumplings

Prep Time: 10 minutes | Cook Time: 15 minutes | Serves: 24

1 medium sweet potato
¼ head cabbage, cut small
1 bunch kale, washed, ribs removed and cut small
2 pieces seitan, cut small
4 ounces firm tofu, cut into small blocks
24 gyoza skins
1 cup vegetable broth
1 dash garlic powder
1 dash onion powder
Salt and soy sauce, to taste
1 tablespoon sesame oil

1. Use some soy sauce and sesame oil, sauté the kale and cabbage in a large wok until tender. 2. Briefly pulse in a food processor and place in a bowl. 3. Pulse the sweet potatoes in the food processor. 4. Add to the cabbage/kale mixture in the bowl. 5. Sauté seitan and tofu in the wok until done for 5 minutes with the soy sauce. Pulse in a food processor and place into the bowl. 6. Season the mixture with the onion and garlic powders, salt, scallions, more sesame oil, and soy sauce to taste. Mix very well. 7. Fill about 1-1.5 teaspoons filling into the gyoza skins and place on a plate. 8. Heat a pan and add 1-2 teaspoons peanut oil. 9. Place the dumplings in the pan and cook until brownish. Add the vegetable broth, cook, and cover for about 6 minutes until broth is absorbed. 10. Plate with a splash each of soy sauce, rice vinegar, and sesame oil. Serve.

Homemade Fried Eggs with Peas

Prep Time: 10 minutes | Cook Time: 15 minutes | Serves: 4

5 large eggs, at room temperature
Kosher salt and ground white pepper, to taste
½ cup thinly sliced shiitake mushroom caps
½ cup frozen peas, thawed
2 scallions, chopped
2 teaspoons sesame oil
½ cup low-sodium chicken broth
1½ tablespoons oyster sauce
1 tablespoon Shaoxing rice wine
½ teaspoon sugar
2 tablespoons light soy sauce
1 tablespoon cornstarch
3 tablespoons vegetable oil
Cooked rice for serving

1. In a large bowl, whisk the eggs with a pinch each of salt and white pepper. Stir in the mushrooms, peas, scallions, and sesame oil. Set aside. 2. Make the sauce by simmering the chicken broth, oyster sauce, rice wine, and sugar in a small saucepan over medium heat. 3. Whisk the light soy and cornstarch in a small glass measuring cup until the cornstarch is completely dissolved. 4. Add the cornstarch mixture into the sauce while whisking constantly and cook for 3 to 4 minutes, until the sauce becomes thick enough to coat the back of the spoon. Cover and set aside. 5. Heat a wok over medium-high heat. 6. Place in the vegetable oil and swirl to coat the base of the wok. 7.Add the egg mixture and cook, swirling and shaking the wok until the bottom side is golden. 8. Slide the omelet out of the pan onto a plate and invert over the wok or turn over with a spatula to cook the other side until golden. 9. Slide the omelet out onto a serving platter and serve.

Marinated Shrimp Dumplings with Bamboo Shoots

Prep Time: 10 minutes | Cook Time: 8 minutes | Serves: 4

½ pound raw shrimp, peeled, deveined
1 teaspoon oyster sauce
1 tablespoon vegetable oil
¼ teaspoon white pepper
1 teaspoon sesame oil
¼ teaspoon salt
1 teaspoon sugar
½ teaspoon ginger, minced
¼ cup bamboo shoots, chopped
12 dumpling wrappers

1. Blend the shrimp with all the filling ingredients (except bamboo shoots) in a blender. 2. Add the bamboo shoots to the blended filling and mix well. Cover and refrigerate this filling for 1 hour. 3. Meanwhile, spread the dumpling wrappers on the working surface. Divide the shrimp filling at the center of each dumpling wrapper. 4. Wet the edges of the dumplings and bring all the edges of each dumpling together. 5. Pinch and seal the edges of the dumplings to seal the filling inside. 6. Boil the water in a suitable pot with a steamer basket placed inside. Add the dumplings to the steamer, cover, and steam for 6 minutes. 7. Meanwhile, heat about 2 tablespoons of oil in a Mandarin wok. 8. Sear the dumpling for 2 minutes until golden. 9. Serve warm.

Veggie and Pork Rolls

Prep Time: 1 hour 10 minutes | Cook Time: 10 minutes | Serves: 20

8 ounces bamboo shoots
1 cup wood ear mushroom
4 teaspoons vegetable oil
3 large eggs
1 teaspoon sugar
14-ounce egg roll wrappers
1 egg white
1-pound roasted pork
2 green onions
2½ teaspoons soy sauce
4 cups oil for frying
1 medium head cabbage
1 carrot
1 teaspoon salt

1. Heat the wok and add one tablespoon oil. Add the beaten egg in the oil and cook for 2 minutes on low heat. 2. Change side and cook for another 1 minute. Set aside and let it cool and slice into thin strips. 3. Add the vegetable oil in a wok and heat the remaining ingredients until vegetables are fully cooked. 4. Add the sliced egg in the vegetables and refrigerate for 1 hour. Cover with plastic to avoid drying. 5. Serve.

Healthy Vegetable Dumplings

Prep Time: 10 minutes | Cook Time: 35 minutes | Serves: 12

12 Dumpling wrappers

Filling:

3 tablespoons oil
1 tablespoon ginger, minced
1 large onion, chopped
2 cups shiitake mushrooms, chopped
1½ cups cabbage, shredded
1½ cups carrot, shredded
1 cup garlic chives, chopped
½ teaspoon white pepper
2 teaspoons sesame oil
3 tablespoons Shaoxing wine
2 tablespoon soy sauce
1 teaspoon sugar
Salt, to taste

1. Sauté onion with oil in a Mandarin wok until soft. 2. Stir in the ginger, cabbage, mushrooms, garlic and the rest of the ingredients. 3. Sauté for about 7–10 minutes until veggies are cooked and soft. 4. Allow the filling to cool and spread the dumpling wrappers on the working surface. 5. Divide the mushroom filling at the center of each dumpling wrapper. Wet the edges of the dumplings and bring all the edges of each dumpling together. 6. Pinch and seal the edges of the dumplings to seal the filling inside. 7. Boil the water in a suitable pot with a steamer basket placed inside. 8. Add the dumplings to the steamer, cover and steam for 23 minutes. 9. Meanwhile, heat about 2 tablespoons of oil in a Mandarin wok. 10. Sear the dumpling for 2 minutes until golden. 11. Serve warm.

Breakfast Fried Egg Rice

Prep Time: 30 minutes | Cook Time: 10 minutes | Serves: 4

Red chilies, two
Jalapeno, one large
Sliced green onions, half cup
White peppercorns, one teaspoon
Cilantro, one cup
Fresh ginger, one tablespoon
Fish sauce, one tablespoon
Soy sauce, one tablespoon
Chinese 5 spice, half teaspoon
Chili garlic sauce, two tablespoon
Fresh cilantro leaves, half cup
Fresh basil leaves, a quarter cup
Chicken broth, one can
Minced lemongrass, one teaspoon
Egg, one large
Cooked rice, as required

1. Add all the ingredients of the curry into a wok. 2. Add the chicken broth and sauces into the mixture. 3. Cook your dish for ten minutes. 4. Add the cooked rice into the mixture. 5. Mix the rice well and cook it for five minutes. 6. Add the eggs into the wok by pushing the rest of the ingredients to a side. 7. Cook the egg and then mix the rest of ingredients into it. 8. Cook your dish for five minutes. 9. Add the cilantro into the dish. 10. Mix your rice and then dish it out. 11. Your dish is ready to be served.

Buttered Banana Breakfast

Prep Time: 30 minutes | Cook Time: 10 minutes | Serves: 4

All-purpose flour, one cup
Mashed bananas, one cup
Butter, half cup
Sugar, half cup
Baking powder, one cup
Rum extract, one tablespoon
Milk, one cup
Almond extract, one tablespoon
Heavy ceam

1. Take a medium bowl and place the butter and mashed bananas in it. 2. Add the one cup flour and oats. 3. Mix them well. 4. Take a large bowl and add the heavy cream into it. 5. Add the sugar, salt, and milk. 6. Mix them well. 7. Add the baking powder in the mixture. 8. Add the eggs and almond extract together. 9. Stir it for few minutes. 10. Steam the mixture in a wok for one hour. 11. Your dish is ready to be served.

Classic Chinese Tea Eggs

Prep Time: 10 minutes | Cook Time: 4 hours 10 minutes | Serves: 8

8 eggs
1 teaspoon salt
3 cups water
1 tablespoon soy sauce
1 tablespoon black soy sauce
¼ teaspoon salt
2 tablespoons black tea leaves
2 pods star anise
1 (2 inches) piece cinnamon stick
1 tablespoon tangerine zest

1. Get your eggs boiling in the water with one teaspoon of salt. 2. Once the mix is boiling, set the heat to low and let the contents simmer for 25 minutes. 3. Now remove the liquids, and once the eggs have cooled, break the shells with a fork. But do not take off the shells. 4. In a wok, get the following boiling: tangerine zest, soy sauce, 3 cups water, cinnamon, anise, black soy sauce, tea leaves, and salt. 5. Once the mix is boiling, place a lid on the wok, set the heat to low, and let the content cook for 4 hours. 6. After the cooking time has elapsed, shut the heat, add your eggs, and let the mix sit overnight. 7. Serve and enjoy.

Garlic Carrot Mushroom Dumplings with Sauce

Prep Time: 10 minutes | Cook Time: 20 minutes | Serves: 9

45 dumpling wrappers
2 teaspoons potato starch
Filling:
4 cloves garlic
1 tablespoon light soy sauce
½ teaspoon salt
1-pound carrots
3 large eggs
1 cup bamboo shoots
1 cup shiitake mushrooms
2 slices ginger
3 tablespoons sesame oil
¼ teaspoon white pepper powder
Sauce:
2 teaspoons light soy sauce
2 tablespoons black vinegar
2 teaspoons chili oil

1. Wash the shiitake mushroom and add the hot water to it. Wait for 30 minutes until the mushrooms tenderize. 2. Dry the mushrooms and cut them into small pieces. 3. Take a walk and fry the mushrooms in 1 tablespoon oil—Cook for 5 minutes. 4. Add the ginger, garlic, and carrot and cook for 1 minute. 5. Add 1 cup of water to the blender and blend the mushroom mixture. 6. Transfer to pan and cook until carrots soften. Add the eggs and cook for 2 minutes. 7. Add the soy sauce, bamboo shoots, salt, and white pepper. Mix and set aside. 8. Combine the potato starch with the water and brush on dumpling wraps. 9. Add one tablespoon mixture overwraps and seal dumplings. 10. Mix all ingredients of the sauce and stir until combined. 11. Steam the dumplings for 8 to 10 minutes and serve with sauce.

Traditional Breakfast Poha

Prep Time: 30 minutes | Cook Time: 50 minutes | Serves: 5

Brown rice, one cup
Tomatoes, two
Red bell pepper, one tablespoon
Cooking oil, one cup
Garlic powder, one tablespoon
Ginger, one tablespoon
Sesame oil, one tablespoon
Peanuts, one cup
Curry leaves, three
Cumin seeds, half tablespoon
Red chili, to serve
Green onions, two
Salt, to taste
Black pepper, to taste

1. Cook the brown rice in rice cooking wok. 2. Drain the brown rice once they are cooked. 3. Add the ginger, garlic powder, and pepper. 4. Cook it for one minute with continuous stirring. 5. Add the green onions into the mixture. 6. Cook it for few minutes. 7. Add the curry leaves and cumin seeds into the mixture. 8. Add the peanuts into the dish. 9. Cook the ingredients well. 10. Add the cooked rice into the whole mixture. 11. Simmer until the poha is cooked. 12. Your dish is ready to be serve.

Tasty Bacon and Egg Fried Rice

Prep Time: 30 minutes | Cook Time: 10 minutes | Serves: 4

Red chilies, two
Jalapeno, one large
Sliced green onions, half cup
White peppercorns, one teaspoon
Cilantro, one cup
Fresh ginger, one tablespoon
Fish sauce, one tablespoon
Soy sauce, one tablespoon
Chinese 5 spice, half teaspoon
Chili garlic sauce, two tablespoon
Fresh cilantro leaves, half cup
Fresh basil leaves, a quarter cup
Chicken broth, one can
Minced lemongrass, one teaspoon
Egg, one large
Bacon slices, half cup
Cooked rice, as required

1. Add all the ingredients of the curry into a wok. 2. Cook the bacon strips and chop them. 3. Add the chicken broth and sauces into the mixture. 4. Cook the dish for ten minutes. 5. Add the cooked rice into the mixture. 6. Mix the rice well and cook it for five minutes. 7. Add the egg into the wok by pushing the rest of the ingredients to a side. 8. Add the bacon and mix the rest of ingredients into it. 9. Cook the dish for five more minutes. 10. Add the cilantro into the dish. 11. Mix your rice and dish it. 12. Your dish is ready to be served.

Healthy Breakfast Omelet

Prep Time: 30 minutes | Cook Time: 10 minutes | Serves: 4

Crab rolls, five
Mushrooms, two
Onions, half cup
Rice wine, one tablespoon
Black pepper, to taste
Salt, to taste
Starch, a quarter teaspoon
Kohlrabi, one cup
Ginger, one slice
Soy sauce, one tablespoon
Oil, one tablespoon
Cilantro, as required

1. Beat the eggs with the water, black pepper, and salt. 2. Add the oil to a wok and place in the beaten eggs. 3. Sprinkle the vegetables on the top. 4. Add the rest of the ingredients on top of the egg mixture. 5. Fold in the egg and cook it on both sides. 6. When the eggs are done, dish them out. 7. Add on top of the eggs the chopped cilantro leaves. 8. Your dish is ready to be served.

Sweet Egg Tarts

Prep Time: 15 minutes | Cook Time: 25 minutes | Serves: 3

Milk, two cups
White sugar, half cup
Salt, one teaspoon
Eggs, two
Lemon extract, one teaspoon
Almond extract, one teaspoon
All-purpose flour, two cups
Butter, one cup
Dry yeast, one cup

1. Take a medium bowl and place the butter inside. 2. Add the one cup flour and combine well. 3. Then refrigerate it. 4. Take a large bowl and add the yeast into it. 5. Add the sugar, salt, and milk. 6. Mix them well. 7. Mix the warm milk mixture with the flour and yeast. 8. Add the lemon extract, eggs, and almond extract together. 9. Stir for few minutes. 10. Then knead it in the flour until the dough is formed. 11. Place the butter on the dough and fold it in the plastic wrap. 12. Refrigerate for thirty minutes. 13. Make the tarts of the dough roll. 14. Steam them in a wok for ten minutes. 15. Your dish is ready to be served.

Delicious Siri Lankan Spicy Breakfast Omelet

Prep Time: 15 minutes | Cook Time: 35 minutes | Serves: 2

Green onion, one cup
Red chili, one teaspoon
Garlic clove, one
Mixed garam masala, one tablespoon
Ginger, two tablespoon
Red sauce, two tablespoon
Eggs, three
Tomatoes, half cup
Softened butter, one tablespoon
Coconut milk, one cup
Black pepper, one tablespoon
Salt, to taste

1. Take a large wok. 2. Heat the wok and add the butter inside. 3. When the butter melts, place in the chopped red onion. 4. cook the onion and add the ginger into the wok. 5. When the color of garlic and ginger changes, add the tomatoes into the mixture. 6. Add the red sauce, salt, and black pepper into the mixture. 7. When the ingredients are cooked enough, reduce the heat. 9. In a small bowl, add the eggs and coconut milk. 8. Beat the mixture well and add it into the wok. 9. Do not mix the ingredients. 10. When the egg mixture solidifies a little, flip it over. 11. Cook both sides of omelet to golden brown color. 12 When the eggs are done, dish them out. 13. Garnish the eggs with the cilantro. 14. Your dish is ready to be served.

Cinnamon Red Bean Bun

Prep Time: 50 minutes | Cook Time: 30 minutes | Serves: 4

Red beans, half pound
Thin soy sauce, one tablespoon
Cinnamon powder, half tablespoon
White sugar, one tablespoon
Sweet vinegar, one tablespoon
Brown powder, one tablespoon
Fresh shallot, half tablespoon
Milk, one cup
Vegetable oil, one tablespoon
All-purpose flour, one cup
Whole wheat flour, half cup
Salt, to taste
Water, to kneed
Yeast, one cup

1. Take a bowl and place the flour into it. 2. Then add the yeast and sugar into it. 3. Add the lukewarm water in it. 4. Set aside for half an hour. 5. In another bowl, take the whole wheat flour. 6. Add the yeast dough in it. 7. Then add the salt and some water in it. 8. Then mix the ingredients to form a soft dough. 9. Kneed it for ten minutes. 10. Meanwhile, grind the red beans. 11. Mix them with the soy sauce, sweet vinegar, sugar, and salt. 12. Make the round forms of dough with the oil. 13. Then bake the buns for ten minutes. 14. Once the buns are steamed, take them out. 15. You can serve the red beans buns.

Sweet Coconut Bun

Prep Time: 50 minutes | Cook Time: 30 minutes | Serves: 4

Sweet coconut, half pound
Thin soy sauce, one tablespoon
Cinnamon powder, half tablespoon
White sugar, one tablespoon
Sweet vinegar, one tablespoon
Brown powder, one tablespoon
Milk, one cup
Vegetable oil, one tablespoon
All-purpose flour, one cup
Whole wheat flour, half cup
Salt, to taste
Water, to kneed
Yeast, one cup

1. Take a bowl and place the flour into it. 2. Then add the yeast and sugar into it. 3. Add the lukewarm water in it. 4. Set aside for half an hour. 5. In another bowl, take the whole wheat flour. 6. Add the yeast dough in it. 7. Then add the salt and some water in it. 8. Then mix the ingredients to form a soft dough. 9. Kneed it for ten minutes. 10. Meanwhile, grind the coconut cubes. 11. Mix them with the soy sauce, sweet vinegar, sugar, and salt. 12. Make the round forms of dough with the oil. 13. Then bake the buns for ten minutes. 14. Once the buns are steamed, take them out. 15. You can serve the red beans buns.

Breakfast Fried Egg and Tomatoes

Prep Time: 30 minutes | Cook Time: 10 minutes | Serves: 4

Spring onions, four
Chili, as required
Pepper, to taste
Butter, as required
Salt, to taste
Baby plum tomatoes, four
Eggs, four
Cilantro, half cup

1. Put the butter in a wok. 2. Add the spring onions and chili into the small wok. 3. Cook for a couple of minutes until softened. 4. Whisk the milk and eggs in a bowl. 5. Add the eggs to the wok. 6. Fry the eggs. 7. Add the tomatoes and cilantro leaves on top. 8. Once cooked, dish it out. 9. Your dish is ready to be served.

Nutritious Scrambled Egg with Salmon

Prep Time: 30 minutes | Cook Time: 10 minutes | Serves: 4

Butter, two tablespoon
Heavy cream, half cup
Smoked salmon, half pound
Salt, to taste
Black pepper, to taste
Chopped fresh chives, as required
Eggs, twelve
Onion, one
Chopped garlic, one tablespoon

1. In a large wok, add the butter and let it melt down. 2. Add in the chopped onion. 3. Cook the onion until soft. 4. Add in the garlic. 5. Mix the onions and garlic for two minutes and add in the smoked salmon. 6. Add the eggs and let it cook. 7. Scramble the mixture. 8. Add in the salt and pepper. 9. Add in the heavy cream in the end. 10. When the eggs are done, dish them out. 11. Add the fresh chopped chives on top. 12. Your dish is ready to be served.

Scrambled Eggs with Tomatoes

Prep Time: 10 minutes | Cook Time: 4 minutes | Serves: 3

2 tablespoons avocado oil, or as needed
6 eggs, beaten
4 ripe tomatoes, cut into wedges
2 thinly sliced green onions

1. Heat 1 tablespoon avocado oil in a wok or pan over medium heat. 2. Boil the eggs in the hot oil and stir until mostly cooked through about 1 minute. 3. Transfer the eggs to a plate. 4. Add one tablespoon avocado oil to the wok, cook the tomatoes, and stir until most of the liquid has evaporated about 2 minutes. 5. Return the eggs to the wok and add the green onions. Cook for about 30 more seconds and stir until the eggs are fully cooked. 6. When cooking is up, serve.

Easy Steamed Eggs

Prep Time: 10 minutes | Cook Time: 15 minutes | Serves: 4

3 medium eggs
2 teaspoons Sea salt
1 cup water
To Serve:
Soy sauce
Sesame oil
1 scallion, finely chopped

1. Beat the eggs in a large bowl. Pour the eggs through a sieve into a steam-proof dish. 2. Add the Sea salt to the dish, and whisk it into the eggs. 3. In your wok over high heat, bring the water to a boil. 4. Place a steamer rack or colander with legs in the wok. Carefully place the dish with the eggs in the wok, and cover the dish with a heat-proof plate. 5. Turn the heat to low, and steam the eggs for 15 minutes. 6. Carefully remove the dish, serve, and enjoy.

Meat Breakfast Hash

Prep Time: 10 minutes | Cook Time: 30 minutes | Serves: 4

Coconut oil, two tablespoon
Cinnamon, half tablespoon
Onion, one
Shredded carrots, one cup
Bacon, one pound
Spinach, two cups
Dried thyme, half tablespoon
Powdered ginger, half tablespoon
Powdered garlic, half tablespoon
Zucchini, one cup
Chicken meat, one pound
Turmeric, half tablespoon
Butternut squash, one cup
Sea salt, to taste

1. Heat the coconut oil in a wok. 2. Add the ground bacon. 3. Once cooked, add in the powdered spices. 4. Remove it from the wok and set it aside. 5. Add in the butternut squash, carrots, zucchini, and chicken. 6. Once they turn soft, add in the spinach as well. 7. Add the spices and cook it for five to ten minutes or until the spinach is wilted. 8. Add in the cooked bacon. 9. Mix the dish well and cook for five minutes. 10. Your dish is ready to be served.

Classic Chinese Omelet

Prep Time: 15 minutes | Cook Time: 5 minutes | Serves: 2

Green onion, one cup
Red chili, one tablespoon
Garlic clove, one
Snow peas, trimmed, one cup
Ginger, two tablespoon
Oyster sauce, two tablespoon
Eggs, three
Olive oil, two tablespoon
Coconut milk, one cup
Bean sprouts, one cup

1. Take a wok and heat it. 2. Add the snow peas into it. 3. Cover it with the boiling water for three minutes. 4. Then drain and rinse it with the cold water. 5. Take another bowl and add snow peas into it. 6. Add the bean sprouts and red chili into it and mix well. 7. Take another bowl and add a tablespoon of hot water in it. 8. Add the ginger, garlic, and oyster sauce into it. 9. Combine all the ingredients well. 10. You can add pepper if you like. 11. Wash the wok and heat it. 12. Pour the egg mixture on the wok. 13. Then spread the snow pea mixture over the omelet. 14. Fold in the omelet and cook it on both sides. 15. When the eggs are done, dish them out. 16. Your dish is ready to be served.

Yummy Crispy Omelet

Prep Time: 30 minutes | Cook Time: 10 minutes | Serves: 4

Red chili paste, two tablespoon
Mushrooms, two
Eggs, eight
Onions, half cup
Rice wine, one tablespoon
Black pepper, to taste
Salt, to taste
Green chilies, a quarter teaspoon
Ginger, one slice
Soy sauce, one tablespoon
Oil, one tablespoon
Cilantro, as required

1. Beat the eggs with the red wine, black pepper, and salt. 2. Add the oil to a wok and place in the beaten eggs. 3. Sprinkle the vegetables on top. 4. Add the rest of the ingredients on top of the egg mixture. 5. Fold the eggs and cook it on both sides. 6. When the eggs are done, dish them out. 7. Add on top of the eggs the chopped cilantro leaves. 8. Your dish is ready to be served.

Chapter 2 Vegetables and Sides

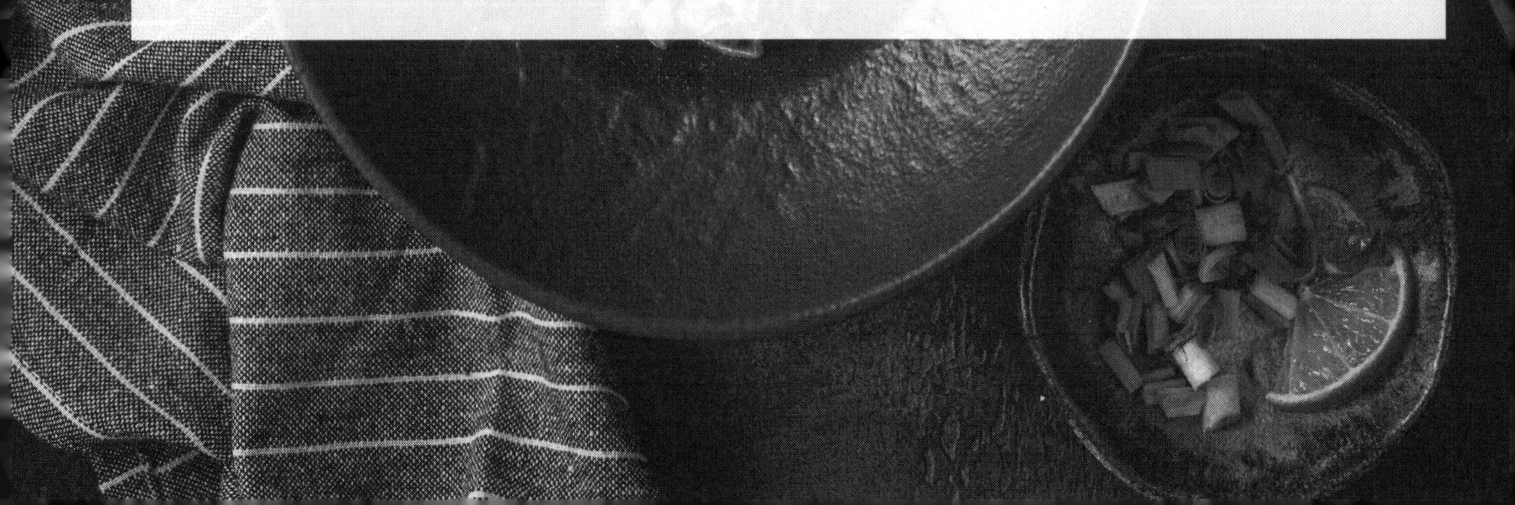

Garlic Lettuce Stir-fry

Prep Time: 2 minutes | Cook Time: 5 minutes | Serves: 4-6

1½ teaspoons soy sauce
1½ teaspoons sesame oil
1 teaspoon rice wine
¾ teaspoon sugar
1 tablespoon peanut or canola oil
3 cloves garlic, peeled and minced
1 head iceberg lettuce, rinsed, dried, and torn into large pieces
Salt and pepper, to taste

1. In a small bowl, stir together the sesame oil, soy sauce, rice wine, and sugar. Set aside. 2. Heat the oil in a wok, skillet, or frying pan over medium-high heat. 3. Stir-fry the garlic until lightly browned. 4. Add the lettuce and stir-fry very briefly until bright in color but still crisp. 5. Stir in the sauce and season with the salt and pepper. 6. Serve

Garlic Bitter Melon with Red Wine Vinegar

Prep Time: 15 minutes | Cook Time: 5 minutes | Serves: 2-4

1 pound bitter melon, seeded and sliced diagonally
Salt, as needed
1 tablespoon minced garlic
½ teaspoon red pepper flakes
2 tablespoons oil
2 tablespoons soy sauce
1 tablespoon red wine or balsamic vinegar
½ teaspoon sugar
½ teaspoon sesame oil

1. Sprinkle the bitter melon slices generously with salt and place in a colander to drain. Let sit for 15 minutes. Wipe dry with the paper towels. 2. In a mortar and pestle or small bowl, mash together the garlic and red pepper flakes. 3. Heat oil in a wok, skillet, or frying pan over medium-high heat. 4. Add the garlic-pepper paste and stir-fry until fragrant (about 30 seconds). 5. Add the bitter melon and stir-fry until color brightens (about 1 minute). 6. Add the soy sauce, vinegar, and sugar. 7. Stir-fry until bitter melon is crisp-tender (about 1–2 minutes). 8. Drizzle with the sesame oil and turn off heat. 9. Serve hot.

Homemade Tso Tofu

Prep Time: 5 minutes | Cook Time: 15 minutes | Serves: 2-3

2 tablespoons soy sauce
1 tablespoon maple syrup
1 (16-ounce) block tofu, extra firm, cut into 1-inch cubes
2 teaspoons cornstarch
3 tablespoons peanut or vegetable oil, divided
1 big head broccoli, broken into florets
Salt and pepper, to taste
2 tablespoons water
2 teaspoons minced ginger
3–4 cloves garlic, minced
4 green onions, roughly chopped
4 pieces fried red chili

For the Sauce:

5–6 tablespoons cornstarch
⅓ cup chicken or vegetable stock
2 tablespoons Chinese black vinegar or balsamic vinegar
2 tablespoons Chinese cooking wine
1 tablespoon light soy sauce
1 tablespoon dark soy sauce
¼ cup sugar

1. In a Ziploc bag, combine the soy sauce and maple syrup. Place in the cubed tofu and let marinate for 10 minutes. 2. Mix the sauce ingredients together in a bowl. Set aside. 3. Heat 2 teaspoons oil in a wok, skillet, or frying pan over medium heat. 4. Add the broccoli and season with the salt and pepper. Stir-fry briefly until color begins to brighten and then add water. Raise heat, if needed, and let steam until tender (about 1 minute). Transfer to serving dish. 5. Wipe any moisture off wok and then add the remaining oil. 6. Drain out the marinade from tofu. Gradually add the cornstarch to tofu in the Ziploc bag, shaking after each addition, to coat. 7. Shake off any excess cornstarch from tofu and add to wok. Let cook until browned underneath and then flip over to brown evenly (about 3–4 minutes). Transfer to a plate. 8. Add more oil to wok, if needed, and stir-fry the garlic, green onions, and dried chilies just until fragrant. 9. Give the prepared sauce a quick stir again and then pours into wok. 10. Cook, with stirring, until thickened. 11. Return the tofu to the wok and toss to coat with the sauce. 12. Pile over the broccoli and serve.

Delicious Vegetables and Tofu in a Peanut Sauce

Prep Time: 20 minutes | Cook Time: 20 minutes | Serves: 4

1 package firm tofu, cubed into bite-sized pieces
2 onions, diced
1 Asian eggplant (long and thin), diced
1 zucchini, diced
2 carrots, halved and sliced
1 red bell pepper, diced
Salt and freshly ground pepper (optional)
Cooked brown rice for serving (optional)
1 tablespoon grapeseed oil

Sauce Ingredients:
4 tablespoons of smooth peanut butter
2 tablespoons tamari
1½ teaspoons white sugar
¼ teaspoon red chili pepper flakes, more if you like it spicier
2 garlic cloves minced
2 teaspoons fresh ginger, minced
1 teaspoon fresh coriander, chopped
1-2 tablespoons of water or more if needed

1. Slice all the vegetables and the tofu in even bite size pieces. 2. In a wok, put 1 tablespoon of grapeseed oil for frying on medium-high heat. Sauté the onions first until tender, add the carrots and peppers and sauté until tender. Add the zucchini and eggplant and fry for another 3 minutes. Place the vegetable on the side of the wok and add the tofu in the center, stirring continuously until it is golden brown, about 3-4 minutes. 3. Combine all the sauce ingredients in a small mixing bowl. Add more water if needed to get the desired consistency. Add the sauce into the wok and stir well. Stir-fry for another 5-10 minutes, or until the flavors are well developed. Season with the salt and freshly ground pepper, if desired. 4. Serve.

Easy Sesame Shiitake Stir-fry

Prep Time: 2 minutes | Cook Time: 10 minutes | Serves: 2

2 tablespoons peanut oil
1 (½-inch) piece ginger, peeled and minced
1 clove garlic, minced
½ pound fresh shiitake mushrooms, sliced
1–2 tablespoons soy sauce
1 tablespoon sesame oil
1 green onion, chopped
2 teaspoons toasted sesame seeds

1. Heat the peanut oil in a wok, skillet, or frying pan over medium high heat. 2. Stir-fry the ginger and garlic until fragrant (about 30 seconds). 3. Add the sliced shiitake and stir-fry until soft and lightly browned (about 2–3 minutes). 4. Add the soy sauce and sesame oil and stir. 5. Continue to stir-fry until most liquid has evaporated. 6. Sprinkle with the sesame seeds and green onion. 7. Serve.

Refreshing Sweet-Sour Veggies

Prep Time: 10 minutes | Cook Time: 15 minutes | Serves: 4

2 tablespoons vegetable oil
4 cloves garlic, minced
1 onion, sliced thinly
½ head cauliflower, chopped into bite-size pieces
1 carrot, peeled and sliced
1 cucumber, cut into bite-size pieces
8 baby corn, sliced
1 cup peas
1 large red bell pepper, sliced
1 tomato, cut into bite-size pieces
¼ fresh pineapple, cut into bite-size chunks

For the Sauce:
3 tablespoons sugar
2 tablespoons lime juice
1 tablespoon fish sauce
1 tablespoon oyster sauce
1 tablespoon light soy sauce

1. Place the sauce ingredients in a saucepan. Stir while heating over medium-low heat. Bring to a simmer. Remove from heat and set aside. 2. Heat the oil in a wok, skillet, or frying pan over medium-high heat. 3. Add the garlic and stir-fry until browned. 4. Add the onion and cook for 1 minute. 5. Add the cauliflower, carrot, cucumber, corn, and peas. Stir-fry for 1 minute. 6. Add the bell pepper and tomato to cook for 1 minute. 7. Pour the prepared sauce into wok. 8. Add the pineapple. 9. Stir and cook 1 minute to heat through and coat well. 10. Serve.

Sesame Tofu and Mushroom

Prep Time: 5 minutes | Cook Time: 15 minutes | Serves: 4

1 (14-ounce) block firm tofu, cut into bite-size cubes
2 tablespoons vegetable oil, divided
1 pound mushrooms, cleaned and sliced
6 green onions, trimmed and cut into 1-inch lengths
1 (2-inch) piece ginger, peeled and sliced
Salt and pepper, to taste
Toasted sesame seeds, for sprinkling

For the Sauce:
2 tablespoons vinegar
2 tablespoons wine
2 tablespoons soy sauce

For Tofu Coating:
1½ teaspoons cornstarch
½ teaspoon red pepper flakes
Pinch of salt
1 tablespoon soy sauce

1. Wrap the tofu cubes in paper towels or a thick kitchen towel and set a weight on top to squeeze out excess liquid. Let sit for at least 15 minutes. 2. Stir together the sauce ingredients in a small bowl. Set aside. 3. In another bowl, combine the Tofu Coating ingredients. Add the pressed tofu and toss to coat. Set aside. 4. Heat 1 tablespoon oil in a wok, skillet, or frying pan over medium-high heat. 5. Add the mushrooms, scallions, and ginger. 6. Season with the salt and pepper and stir-fry for about 5 minutes until tender and slightly browned. Transfer to a plate. 7. Add the remaining oil to wok and raise flame to high. Heat oil until it shimmers. 8. Shake off any excess coating and lay tofu in the wok. Let cook until one side is browned (about 2 minutes). 9. Flip over to brown second side. Carefully loosen the tofu with a spatula, if needed. 10. Pour in the sauce mixture. 11. Return the mushroom mixture to wok and reduce heat. 12. Toss until all ingredients are coated and sauce is thickened. 13. Season with more salt and pepper, if needed, and sprinkle with the sesame seeds. 14. Serve immediately over rice.

Garlic Zucchini Broccoli Stir Fry

Prep Time: 20 minutes | Cook Time: 20 minutes | Serves: 2

6 oz skinless, boneless chicken breast, cut into small pieces
2 tbsp soy sauce
2 tbsp dry sherry
1 tbsp cornstarch
1 tbsp vegetable oil
1 C. broccoli florets, cut into pieces
1 large green bell pepper, cut into squares
1 zucchini, cut into rounds and quartered
3 cloves garlic, minced
½ C. chicken broth
1 tbsp vegetable oil
6 green onions, chopped

1. In a large mixing bowl: Mix in it the chicken, sherry, soy sauce, and cornstarch. 2. Place a large wok over medium heat. Heat 1 tbsp of oil in it. Add the broccoli, bell pepper, zucchini, and garlic. Cook them for 4 minutes. 3. Stir in the broth and put on the lid. Cook them for 7 min. Transfer the mix to a bowl and place it aside. 4. Place a large wok over medium heat. Heat in it the rest of oil. Add the chicken with a pinch of pepper and salt for 7 min. 5. Add the cooked veggies mix. Cook them for 4 min. 6. Serve your stir fry warm. Enjoy.

Spicy Okra Stir-fry

Prep Time: 5 minutes | Cook Time: 5 minutes | Serves: 2

1 tablespoon peanut or vegetable oil
1 teaspoon Sichuan peppercorn
2 dried chili peppers, chopped
7 ounces okra, cut into bite-size pieces
2 teaspoons light soy sauce

1. Heat the oil in a wok, skillet, or frying pan over medium heat. 2. Stir-fry Sichuan peppercorn until dark and fragrant (about 1 minute). Fish out the peppercorns and discard. 3. Add the chili and stir-fry briefly (about 30 seconds). 4. Adjust heat to high. 5. Add the okra and stir-fry to blanch and coat with oil (1 minute). 6. Add the soy sauce. Reduce the heat, if needed. 7. Continue stir-frying until the okra is cooked through (about 3 minutes). 8. Serve hot.

Spicy Garlic Szechuan Eggplant

Prep Time: 5 minutes | Cook Time: 15 minutes | Serves: 2

2 long eggplants
Water, for soaking
1 teaspoon salt, for soaking
2 tablespoons vegetable oil
2 garlic cloves, chopped
2 Thai red hot pepper, finely chopped
2 green onions, white and green separated, chopped
1 (1-inch piece) ginger, peeled and chopped
1 tablespoon broad bean paste
Cilantro, for garnish

For the Sauce:
1 tablespoon light soy sauce
1 tablespoon black vinegar
1 tablespoon cooking wine
2 teaspoons cornstarch
1 teaspoon sugar
1 tablespoon water

1. Dissolve the salt in enough water to cover eggplants. Soak eggplant for 15 minutes. Drain well. 2. In a bowl, stir sauce ingredients together. Set aside. 3. Heat the oil in the wok, skillet, or frying pan over medium-high heat, to shimmering. 4. Add the eggplant and stir-fry until lightly browned and tender (about 3 minutes). Push to the side. 5. Add the garlic, peppers, whites of onion, and ginger. Stir-fry until fragrant. 6. Add broad bean sauce and stir-fry for 1 minute. 7. Toss all ingredients together to coat with bean sauce. 8. Pour in the sauce and stir-fry until eggplant slices are well-coated. 9. Serve garnished with the chopped green onions and cilantro.

Southwest Tofu Scramble

Prep Time: 30 minutes | Cook Time: 10 minutes | Serves: 4

Butter, two tablespoon
Coconut cream, half cup
Chopped tofu, half pound
Salt, to taste
Southwest chili sauce, two tablespoon
Black pepper, to taste
Chopped fresh chives, as required
Eggs, twelve
Onions, one
Chopped garlic, one teaspoon

1. In a large wok, add the butter and let it melt down. 2. Add in the chopped onion. 3. Cook the onion until soft. 4. Add in the garlic. 5. Mix the onions and garlic for two minutes and add in the tofu pieces. 6. Add the eggs and let it cook. 7. Scramble the mixture. 8. Add in the salt and pepper. 9. Add in the coconut cream in the end. 10. When the eggs are done, dish them out. 11. Add the fresh chopped chives on top. 12. Your dish is ready to be served.

Homemade Ginger Sesame Tofu

Prep Time: 30 minutes | Cook Time: 10 minutes | Serves: 4

Sesame seeds, one cup
Jalapeno, one large
Sliced green onions, half cup
Tofu cubes, two cups
White peppercorns, one teaspoon
Cilantro, one cup
Fresh ginger, one teaspoon
Fish sauce, one tablespoon
Soy sauce, one tablespoon
Chinese 5 spice, half teaspoon
Chili garlic sauce, two tablespoon
Fresh cilantro leaves, half cup
Fresh basil leaves, a quarter cup
Vegetable broth, one can
Crushed lemon grass, one teaspoon

1. Add all the ingredients of the sauce into a wok. 2. Add the vegetable broth and sauces into the mixture. 3. Cook your dish for ten minutes. 4. Add the tofu pieces into the mixture once the sauce is ready. 5. Mix the ingredients well and cook it for five minutes. 6. Add the basil leaves and then mix the rest of the ingredients into it. 7. Cook your dish for five more minutes. 8. Add the sesame seeds and cilantro into the dish. 9. Your dish is ready to be served.

Sweet Tomato and Egg Stir-Fry

Prep Time: 30 minutes | Cook Time: 10 minutes | Serves: 4

Sugar, two teaspoon
Medium tomatoes, four
Eggs, four
White pepper, a quarter teaspoon
Water, half cup
Scallions, one
Sesame oil, two teaspoon
Vegetable oil, three tablespoon

1. Heat the wok and add the oil. 2. Add the eggs and mix them. 3. Remove the scrambled eggs into a dish. 4. Add one more tablespoon of oil to the wok, and add the tomatoes and scallions. 5. Stir-fry for one minute, and then add two teaspoons of sugar, half teaspoon salt, and a quarter cup water. 6. Add the cooked eggs in the mixture. 7. Your dish is ready to be served.

Healthy Cabbage Burji and Carrots

Prep Time: 15 minutes | Cook Time: 30 minutes | Serves: 3

Cabbage, one pound
Carrots, one
Tomatoes, two
Red bell pepper, one tablespoon
Cooking oil, one cup
Garlic powder, one tablespoon
Ginger, one tablespoon
Sesame oil, one tablespoon
Corn starch, one teaspoon
Red chili, to serve
Green onions, two
Salt, to taste
Black Pepper, to taste

1. Take a large wok and add oil in it. 2. Heat it over medium high heat. 3. Add the cut up cabbage into it. 4. Add the ginger, garlic powder and pepper. 5. Cook it for one minute with the continuous stirring. 6. Add the green onions into the mixture. 7. Cook it for one minute more. 8. Continue boiling for five minutes until water reduces to minimum level. 9. Add the sauce ingredients in a separate bowl. 10. Add the corn starch in the bowl. 11. Dissolve your entire cornstarch in water and make sure no lumps are formed. 12. Put the cornstarch mixture into the wok and cook well. 13. Cook until your cabbage becomes almost dry and smooth. 14. Your dish is ready to be served with the sauces that you prefer.

Tasty Almond and Vegetable Stir-Fry

Prep Time: 10 minutes | Cook Time: 20 minutes | Serves: 4

Fish sauce, two tablespoon
Soy sauce, half cup
Mixed vegetables, three cups
Tomatoes, two
Cilantro, half cup
Salt and pepper, to taste
Minced ginger, half tablespoon
Vegetable oil, two tablespoon
Red chili peppers, three
Toasted almonds, half cup
Onion, one
Scallions, half cup
Minced garlic, one teaspoon

1. In a large wok, add the shallots and oil. 2. Cook your shallots and then add the ginger and garlic. 3. Cook your ginger and garlic and then add in the mixed vegetables. 4. Stir fry your vegetables. 5. Add all the spices and the rest of the ingredients into your dish except the toasted almonds. 6. When your vegetables are cooked, add the toasted almonds. 7. Cook your dish for five minutes. 8. Garnish your dish with cilantro. 9. Your dish is ready to be served.

Healthy Teriyaki Burgers

Prep Time: 30 minutes | Cook Time: 45 minutes | Serves: 4

½ tbsp peanut oil
½ C. onion (purple)
1 C. zucchini
½ C. red bell pepper
2 eggs
½ tsp ginger (ground)
½ tsp cumin
¼ C. soy sauce
¼ C. teriyaki sauce
¼ C. walnut pieces
1 ½ C. brown rice (cooked)

1. Before you do anything heat the oven on 350 F. 2. Chop the bell pepper with zucchini until they become fine. Mince the onion. 3. Place a large wok on medium heat. Add the oil and heat it. Stir in the onion and cook it for 6 min. 4. Stir in the chopped zucchini with bell pepper to the onion. Cook them for 16 min while stirring occasionally. Turn off the heat and allow the mix to lose heat. 5. Get a mixing bowl: Add the eggs and beat them. Stir in the onion mix with ginger, cumin, soy sauce, teriyaki sauce, walnuts and cooked rice. Mix them well. Shape the mix into 4 burgers. 6. Place the burgers on the baking pan. Cook them in the oven for 8 min on each side. 7. Assemble your burgers with your favorite toppings. Serve them right away. Enjoy.

Japanese Style Spring Stir Fry

Prep Time: 5 minutes | Cook Time: 40 minutes | Serves: 4

4 C. cooked rice or 1 C. uncooked rice
1 C. frozen peas, thawed
2 tbsp carrots, finely diced
2 eggs, beaten
½ C. onion, diced
1 ½ tbsp butter
2 tbsp soy sauce
Salt
Pepper

1. Prepare the rice according to the directions on the package. Drain the rice and place it in the fridge to lose heat. 2. Place a large greased wok over medium heat. Scramble in it the eggs while crumbling them then place them aside. 3. In a large mixing bowl: Place in it the rice with scrambled eggs, peas, scrambled egg, grated carrot, and diced onion. Mix them well. 4. Place a large wok over medium heat. Heat the butter in it until it melts. Add the rice mix with the soy sauce, a pinch of salt, and pepper. 5. Stir fry it for 9 min. Serve your stir fried rice warm. Enjoy.

Homemade Apple Ramen Salad

Prep Time: 15 minutes | Cook Time: 20 minutes | Serves: 10

12 oz. broccoli florets
1 (12 oz.) bags broccoli coleslaw mix
¼ C. sunflower seeds
2 (3 oz.) packages ramen noodles
3 tbsp butter
2 tbsp olive oil
¼ C. sliced almonds
¾ C. vegetable oil
¼ C. brown sugar
¼ C. apple cider vinegar
¼ C. green onion, chopped

1. Place a large wok over medium heat. Heat the oil in it. 2. Press the ramen with the hands to crush it. Stir it in the wok with the almonds. 3. Cook for 6 minutes and then place the wok aside. 4. In a large mixing bowl: Mix in it the broccoli slaw, broccoli, and sunflowers. Add the noodles mix and mix them again. 5. In a small mixing bowl: Combine in it the vegetable oil, apple cider vinegar, brown sugar, and the Ramen noodle seasoning packet to make the vinaigrette. 6. Drizzle the vinaigrette all over the salad and stir it to coat. Serve the salad with the green onions on top. Enjoy.

Delicious Sweet Ramen with Tofu

Prep Time: 10 minutes | Cook Time: 20 minutes | Serves: 1

1 package chicken-flavored ramen noodles
2 C. water
2 tbsp vegetable oil
3 slices tofu, ¼ inch thick
2 C. soy bean sprouts or 2 C. mung bean sprouts
½ small zucchini, thinly sliced
2 green onions, sliced
½ C. sweet green pea pods
Flour
Seasoning salt
Sesame oil

1. Slice each tofu piece into 3 chunks. Dust with some flour. 2. Place a large wok over medium heat. Heat 1 tbsp of oil in it. Cook the tofu for 1 to 2 minutes on each side in it. Drain and place aside. 3. Heat a splash of oil in the same pan. Sauté in it the veggies for 6 minutes. Place aside. 4. Cook the noodles by following the directions on the package. Stir in it the seasoning packet. 5. Place a large wok over medium heat. Heat a splash of oil in it. Cook the bean sprouts for 1 minute in it. 6. Lay the fried bean sprouts in the bottom of serving bowl. Top it with the cooked veggies ramen, and tofu. Serve them hot. Enjoy.

Sweet and Spicy Ramen Stir Fry with Spinach

Prep Time: 10 minutes | Cook Time: 30 minutes | Serves: 4

1 (14 oz.) packages extra firm tofu, cubed
8 tsp soy sauce
2 tbsp vegetable oil
8 oz. shiitake mushrooms, sliced thin
2 tsp Asian chili sauce
3 garlic cloves, minced
1 tbsp grated fresh ginger
3 ½ C. low sodium chicken broth
4 (3 oz.) packages ramen noodles, packets discarded
3 tbsp cider vinegar
2 tsp sugar
1 (6 oz.) bags Baby Spinach

1. Pat the tofu dry with some paper towels. 2. In a mixing bowl: Stir the tofu with 2 tsp of soy sauce in it. 3. Place a large wok over medium heat. Heat 1 tbsp of oil in it. Sauté the tofu for 2 to 3 minutes on each side in it and then drain and place aside. 4. Heat the rest of the oil in the same wok. Sauté the mushroom for 5 minutes in it. Add the garlic, chili sauce, and ginger. Let them cook for 40 seconds. 5. Crush the ramen into pieces. Stir it into the wok with the broth and cook for 3 minutes or until the ramen is done. 6. Add 2 tbsp soy sauce, vinegar, and sugar. Add the spinach and cook them for 2 to 3 minutes or until it welts. 7. Fold the tofu into the noodles and then serve it warm. Enjoy.

Savory Garlic Almond Bean Stir-Fry

Prep Time: 25 minutes | Cook Time: 15 minutes | Serves: 6

1 package whole wheat fettuccine
¼ cup rice vinegar
3 tablespoons reduced-sodium soy sauce
2 tablespoons brown sugar
2 tablespoons fish sauce
1 tablespoon lime juice
Dash of Louisiana-style hot sauce
3 teaspoons canola oil, divided
1 package extra-firm tofu, drained and cut into ½-inch cubes
2 medium carrots, grated
2 cups fresh snow peas, halved
3 garlic cloves, minced
2 large eggs, lightly beaten
2 cups bean sprouts
3 green onions, chopped
½ cup fresh cilantro, minced
¼ cup unsalted peanuts, chopped

1. Cook the fettuccine as directed on the packet. Meanwhile, whisk together the vinegar, brown sugar, soy sauce, fish sauce, lime juice, and spicy sauce in a small bowl until smooth. 2. Heat 2 tablespoons of oil in a large wok over medium-high heat. Cook and stir the tofu until golden brown, about 4 to 6 minutes. 3. Remove from the wok and keep warm. Cook and toss the carrots and snow peas until crisp-tender in the remaining oil, about 3 to 5 minutes. 4. Cook for a further minute after adding the garlic. Add the eggs and cook, stirring constantly, until they're set.Drain the pasta and toss it in with the vegetables. Add the vinegar mixture to the wok after stirring it. 5. Bring the mixture to a boil. Heat through the tofu, bean sprouts, and onions.

Garlic Cabbage Scrambled with Chicken Dice

Prep Time: 15 minutes | Cook Time: 12 minutes | Serves: 6

5 cloves garlic, minced
2 tablespoons fresh ginger, chopped
½ teaspoon red pepper flakes
¼ teaspoon ground cloves
4 tablespoons low-sodium soy sauce, divided
2 tablespoons rice vinegar
1½ tablespoons pure maple syrup
1 small cabbage (about 1–1½ pounds)
2 tablespoons extra-virgin olive oil, divided
1 pound ground chicken
2 cups carrots, shredded
1 small bunch of green onions, finely chopped
½ cup fresh cilantro leaves and tender stems, chopped

1. Combine the garlic, red pepper flakes, ginger, and cloves in a small bowl. Combine 2 teaspoons soy sauce, rice vinegar, and maple syrup in a separate bowl. Set both bowls aside. 2. Cut the cabbage's stem end off. Then, chop it in half from the top of the cabbage to the branch. Place the flat, cut side of each half against the cutting board's surface, then cut each half into quarters. 3. Over medium-high heat, heat a large wok with a tight-fitting lid. Add 1 tablespoon of extra-virgin olive oil. Add the chicken after the pan is hot and shimmering. Cook and break up the meat as it cooks. Add the remaining 2 tablespoons of soy sauce and mix well. Cook for another 5 minutes, or until the meat is fully cooked through and any liquid gathered in the pan has mostly evaporated. Place on a platter or in a dish. 4. In the same wok, place in the remaining 1 tablespoon of oil. Add the cabbage and carrots and cook, turning periodically, for 2 minutes, or until the cabbage begins to wilt. 5. Combine the soy sauce and spice combination in a mixing bowl. Add to the wok and cook, covered, for 1 minute over high heat, until the cabbage is thoroughly wilted but not mushy. 6. Remove the lid and mix in the green onion and cilantro. Cook for another 30 seconds. 7. Serve hot.

Sesame Broccoli with Soy-Oyster Sauce

Prep Time: 5 minutes | Cook Time: 10 minutes | Serves: 4

1 pound broccoli florets
¼ cup chicken broth
1 tablespoon oyster sauce
1 tablespoon dark soy sauce
1 teaspoon sugar
¼ teaspoon sesame oil
Salt, to taste
1 teaspoon cornstarch
4 teaspoons water
2 tablespoons white sesame seeds for garnish

1. Bring a large pot of the salted water to a boil. Cook for 2 to 3 minutes, until the broccoli is cooked but still crisp. 2. Remove the broccoli and immerse it in ice-cold water for a few seconds. 3. Drain all of the water from the broccoli. Place in a serving bowl and set aside. 4. Bring the granulated sugar, chicken broth, dark soy sauce, oyster sauce, and sesame oil to a boil in a small saucepan, constantly stirring to dissolve the sugar. Season the mixture with salt to taste. 5. Dissolve the cornstarch in the water in a small bowl to make a slurry. 6. Add the cornstarch slurry and whisk it continually until it thickens to thicken the sauce. 7. Pour the sauce over the broccoli that has been blanched. Enjoy.

Japanese Flavorful Dashi Omelet

Prep Time: 15 minutes | Cook Time: 10 minutes | Serves: 6

4 eggs
¼ C. prepared dashi stock
1 tbsp white sugar
1 tsp mirin
½ tsp soy sauce
½ tsp vegetable oil, or more as needed

1. In a large mixing bowl: Beat the eggs in it well. Add the dashi stock, sugar, mirin, and soy sauce. Mix them well. 2. Place a large wok over medium heat. Heat the oil in it. Pour enough of the eggs mix to make a thin layer to cover the bottom of the pan. 3. Cook it until it becomes firm from the bottom. Roll the omelet and until you reach the side of the wok and leave it there. 4. Grease the wok again with oil and pour in it another thin layer of the eggs mix. Cook it until it becomes firm and roll it to the side on the first egg roll. 5. Repeat the process with the remaining egg mix until it is all used. 6. Serve your omelet warm. Enjoy.

Yummy Sichuan Eggplant in Sauce

Prep Time: 30 minutes | Cook Time: 10 minutes | Serves: 4

2 medium Chinese eggplants

For the Sauce:

4½ teaspoons dark soy sauce
4½ teaspoons light soy sauce
1 tablespoon Chinese red rice vinegar
1 tablespoon Chinese rice wine
½ teaspoon sugar
⅓ cup vegetable broth
1 pinch freshly ground black pepper
¼ teaspoon cornstarch
1 tablespoon vegetable oil
2 teaspoons garlic, minced
1 teaspoon ginger, minced
1 green onion, white and green parts, finely chopped
1 tablespoon chili garlic sauce
1 tablespoon water

1. Bring a large pot of the salted water to a boil. 2. Prepare the eggplant as the water is coming to a boil. Cut the ends off the eggplant and then cut it in half crosswise. Each half should be quartered lengthwise. 3. Cut the eggplant slices diagonally into ¾-inch thick pieces by lining them up from left to right. 4. Cook the eggplant for 2 to 3 minutes in the boiling water. 5. Using paper towels, drain the eggplant. 6. Mix the dark and light soy sauces, vinegar, rice wine (or dry sherry), sugar, and chicken broth in a small bowl. Set aside. 7. Combine the black pepper and cornstarch in a separate small bowl. 8. Heat 1 tablespoon of oil in the wok over medium-high heat. Add the ginger, garlic, and green onion to the heated oil. 9. Stir-fry for a total of 10 seconds. 10. Add the chili garlic sauce and combine well. 11. Add in the eggplant and toss for a minute to combine everything. Re-stir the sauce and swirl it into the pan, swirling constantly. Reduce to medium-low heat, cover, and cook for 10 minutes, or until the eggplant is soft. 12. Combine the cornstarch and water in a small cup. 13. To thicken, pour the cornstarch slurry into the center of the pan and swirl quickly. The dish is finished once the slurry has reduced. Serve immediately.

Simple Daikon Radish

Prep Time: 5 minutes | Cook Time: 25 minutes | Serves: 4

1 pound daikon radish
1 slice ginger
1 cup water or stock
1 tablespoon oyster sauce
½ teaspoon salt (or to taste)
¼ teaspoon sugar
¼ teaspoon ground white pepper
1 scallion, chopped
¼ teaspoon sesame oil

1. Cut the daikon into bite-sized slices that are ½-inch thick. Combine the ginger, water or stock, oyster sauce, salt, sugar, and ground white pepper in a wok. Toss in the daikon. 2. Bring everything to a boil, then turn down the heat to medium-low. Cook and stir periodically, for 20 minutes, or until the daikon is fork-tender. 3. Add the chopped scallion and a few drops of sesame oil just before serving. Serve after thorough mixing.

Bok Choy and Broccoli Stir Fry in Oyster Sauce

Prep Time: 10 minutes | Cook Time: 30 minutes | Serves: 4

2 bunches broccoli
⅓ cup of oyster sauce
2 tablespoons of soy sauce
½ teaspoon white sugar
3 tablespoons of vegetable oil
3 garlic cloves
1 red chili
4 Bok choy bunches

1. Cut each bunch of broccoli in half to remove the stems from the leaves. Set aside the leaves. 2. Combine the oyster sauce, soy sauce and white sugar in a small bowl. In a wok, heat the vegetable oil over high heat. 3. Stir-fry for approximately 30 seconds after adding the garlic and chili. Stir in the Chinese broccoli stems for approximately two minutes. 4. Toss in the wok the broccoli leaves, Bok choy, and oyster sauce, then stir-fry for another two minutes, or until the greens have wilted somewhat. 5. Take the wok off the heat and serve.

Healthy Veggie Bowl

Prep Time: 10 minutes | Cook Time: 20 minutes | Serves: 2

1 Daikon, cut it into very thin strips
½ cup of vinegar
1 tablespoon of sugar
1 teaspoon chili flakes
Salt and pepper, to taste

For Mushrooms Oyster:

9 ounces of mushrooms, oysters
1 tablespoon of tamari
1 tablespoon of Sriracha
½ teaspoon of sugar
1 teaspoon of vinegar
½ teaspoon of sesame oil

1. Add vinegar, ½ cup of water, sugar, salt, and chili flakes in a wok, and bring it to a gentle boil. After 10 minutes, remove it from the flame. 2. In the above wok, put the sliced daikon. Put the lid on it and put it in the fridge for at least one day before use. Let it cool. 3. Mix all the ingredients of mushroom oyster in a pan. 4. Let it marinate for 15 minutes. Set it aside. 5. Heat a frying pan on moderate-high heat after the mushrooms have been marinated. 6. With a little bit of oil, clean its surface and put the mushrooms on it once the pan is heated. 7. Grill the mushrooms until they are golden-brown and cooked through. Make sure you keep an eye on them all the way so they do not roast. 8. Serve.

Sweet Chili Tofu Stir Fry with Bok Choy

Prep Time: 10 minutes | Cook Time: 20 minutes | Serves: 4

1½ pound baby Bok choy, sliced lengthways
30 ounces firm tofu, cubed
1 large red onion, peeled and sliced thinly
6 garlic cloves, peeled and crushed
⅓ cup sweet chili sauce
3 tablespoon soy sauce
3 tablespoon peanut oil
3 tablespoon Keycap Manis
1½ tablespoon chopped fresh ginger
1½ tablespoon toasted sesame seeds
3 teaspoon sesame oil

1. Combine the ginger and tofu, then add the soy sauce and set aside for 15 minutes. 2. Place the wok over a high flame and add half the peanut oil. Stir in the onion until tender. 3. Drain the tofu and add to the wok, followed by the garlic. 4. Stir fry for 3 minutes, then transfer to a plate. Wipe the wok clean and place over high flame. 5. Add the remaining peanut oil, then sauté the Bok choy until wilted. 6. Add the sesame oil, chili sauce, and keycap Mains.

Garlic Asparagus Stir-Fry

Prep Time: 15 minutes | Cook Time: 10 minutes | Serves: 5

1 teaspoon cornstarch
1 teaspoon sugar
3 tablespoons cold water
2 tablespoons reduced-sodium soy sauce
1 teaspoon sesame oil
4 cups fresh broccoli florets
2 tablespoons canola oil
1 large sweet red pepper, cut into 1-inch chunks
1 small onion, cut into thin wedges
2 garlic cloves, minced
1 tablespoon fresh ginger root, minced
¼ cup slivered almonds, toasted

1. Combine the cornstarch and sugar in a small bowl. Set aside after mixing in the water, soy sauce, and sesame oil until smooth. 2. For 3 minutes in the wok, stir-fry the broccoli in heated oil. Stir in the pepper, onion, garlic, and ginger and cook for 2 minutes. 3. Reduce the temperature. Stir the soy sauce mixture into the vegetables, along with the nuts. Cook and stir for 2 minutes, or until the sauce has thickened. 4. Serve.

Salty Garlic Asparagus Stir-Fry

Prep Time: 10 minutes | Cook Time: 7 minutes | Serves: 3

¼ cup chicken broth
2½ tablespoons oyster sauce
½ teaspoon granulated sugar
Freshly ground black pepper, to taste
1 teaspoon cornstarch
2 teaspoons water
2 tablespoons peanut oil
1½ teaspoons fresh ginger, minced
1 teaspoon garlic, finely chopped
½ pound asparagus, washed, trimmed, and cut diagonally into 1½-inch strips
¼ cup water
1 cup mushrooms, sliced
1 red bell pepper, deseeded, and cut into thin strips
1 teaspoon Chinese rice wine, or dry sherry, as needed
¼ to ½ teaspoon Asian sesame oil

1. Combine the chicken broth, oyster sauce, sugar, and black pepper in a small bowl or measuring cup. Dissolve the cornstarch in the water in a separate small bowl. 2. Heat the wok and drizzle in the oil, turning it around to coat the bottom part of the pan. Add the garlic and ginger to the heated oil, and stir for 10 seconds or until fragrant. Stir in the asparagus and cook for 1 minute. Add the water, cover, and steam for 1 to 2 minutes, or until almost all of the water has been absorbed. 3. The asparagus should be pushed to the sides of the wok. In the center, place the mushrooms and bell pepper. Stir-fry for a minute while sprinkling a little rice wine or dry sherry over the mushrooms. Push the bell pepper and mushrooms to the sides of the wok. 4. Give the sauce a short toss before pouring it into the wok's center. Stir together the cornstarch and water and immediately pour them into the sauce to thicken it. Stir to incorporate the veggies in the thickened sauce once it has reduced. Add the sesame oil and mix well. Serve hot.

Chapter 3 Poultry

Nutritious Chicken and Green Beans

Prep Time: 6 minutes | Cook Time: 10 minutes | Serves: 4

1 pound chicken thighs or breasts, boneless, skinless, sliced thinly against the grain
2 tablespoons vegetable oil, divided
6 scallions, ends trimmed, cut into 1-inch pieces
1 (2-inch) piece ginger, sliced
¾ pound green beans, trimmed and halved
Salt, to taste
Toasted peanuts, for sprinkling

For the Marinade:
1½ teaspoons cornstarch
½ teaspoon red pepper flakes, or to taste
Salt, to taste
1 tablespoon soy sauce

For the Sauce:
2 tablespoons soy sauce, divided
2 tablespoons seasoned rice vinegar
2 tablespoons Chinese cooking wine

1. Toss the marinade ingredients in a bowl, add chicken slices and toss. 2. Stir the sauce ingredients together in a small bowl. Set aside. 3. In a wok, skillet, or frying pan, heat 1 tablespoon oil to shimmering. 4. Add the scallion and ginger. Stir-fry until browned (about 2 minutes). 5. Place in the green beans and a pinch of salt, tossing until crisp-tender (about 4 minutes). Transfer veggies to a plate, keeping wok hot. 6. Add the remaining oil and adjust heat to high. 7. When the oil is almost smoking, lay the chicken on wok and let cook until underside is browned (about 1 minute). 8. Stir-fry for 1–2 minutes, or until evenly browned. 9. Stir in the sauce and veggies. 10. Toss until the sauce is thickened (about 30 seconds). 11. Remove from heat and season with more salt, if needed. 12. Sprinkle with the toasted nuts and serve with rice.

Ginger Onion Chicken and Bok Choy Stir-fry

Prep Time: 20 minutes | Cook Time: 10 minutes | Serves: 4

4 boneless chicken breast, brushed with olive oil and thinly sliced
1 red onion, diced
2 heads of bok choy, thinly sliced
2 teaspoons sesame seeds
2 tablespoons ground coriander
2 tablespoons fresh ginger, minced
¼ cup chicken stock
3 tablespoons oyster sauce
2 tablespoons grapeseed oil
2 green onions, sliced
Rice for serving (optional)

1. After you brush the chicken with olive oil, coat them with sesame seeds. 2. On high, heat the oil in the wok. Add the ginger to cook for 2 minutes, stirring frequently. 3. Add the red onion and sauté until tender. Push the onions and ginger to the sides of the wok. Then add chicken and sauté for 2 minutes until the chicken starts to brown and loses its pink color. 4. Add the bok choy, oyster sauce, coriander, green onions, and vegetable stock. Sauté for 2-3 minutes or until tender and chicken is cooked through. 5. Serve with rice if desired and enjoy!

Sesame Basil Chicken with Bell Peppers

Prep Time: 15 minutes | Cook Time: 20 minutes | Serves: 4

1½ tablespoons grapeseed oil
4 skinless boneless chicken breast halves, cut thinly
3 bell peppers, thinly sliced
1 large onion, diced
1 teaspoon fresh ginger
2 garlic cloves, minced
½ cup fresh basil
2 tablespoons tamari sauce
2 green onions, sliced
1½ teaspoons sesame oil
1 tablespoon sesame seeds
Rice for serving (optional)

1. Heat the grapeseed oil in the wok on medium-high and sauté the onion until translucent, about 1 minute. Add peppers and sauté until soft, about 2-3 minutes. Push to the sides of the wok. 2. Put in the chicken in the center and cook for 5-6 minutes or cooked through. 3. Add the basil, sesame oil, tamari sauce, and green onions. Stir fry for 1-2 more minutes. Remove from heat and add sesame seeds. Mix well. 4. Serve over rice if desired.

Fresh Pineapple Chicken Stir-fry

Prep Time: 15 minutes | Cook Time: 10 minutes | Serves: 6

1½ pounds skinless boneless chicken breasts, thinly sliced
Salt and black pepper
2 carrots, thinly sliced
2 onions, chopped
1 cup broccoli, chopped into florets
1 cup fresh pineapple, diced
¼ cup cashews, chopped finely
1 tablespoon honey
2 teaspoons sesame oil
1 teaspoon fresh ginger, minced
2 tablespoons water
2 tablespoons grapeseed oil
Cooked rice for serving (optional)

1. Season the chicken with the salt and pepper. 2. Mix the honey, sesame oil, cashews, ginger, and water. Set aside. 3. Heat the oil on medium-high in the wok. Add the onions and sauté until soft, about 1 minutes. 3. Add the carrots and broccoli and cook until tender. Turn the heat down to medium. 4. Put the vegetables on the side of the wok and cook the chicken for 5 minutes. 5. Add the pineapple and mix everything in the middle with the sauce and cook until warm, about 1-2 minutes. 6. Serve with the rice if desired and enjoy!

Garlic Chicken with Sesame and Leek

Prep Time: 5 minutes | Cook Time: 15 minutes | Serves: 4

1 tablespoon vegetable oil
2 teaspoons sesame oil
1½ pounds boneless, skinless chicken breast, cut into bite-size pieces
2 cloves garlic, minced
1 leek, cut into thin half-moons, rinsed and drained on paper towels
2 tablespoons soy sauce
1 tablespoon Mirin or Chinese cooking wine
1 teaspoon sugar
2 tablespoons toasted sesame seeds
Salt and pepper, to taste
Green onions, chopped, for garnish

1. Heat the vegetable and sesame oil in a wok, skillet, or frying pan over high heat. 2. Swirl the oil to coat the wok and add the chicken (you may have to do this in batches). 3. Stir-fry the chicken until browned on the outside. 4.Stir in the garlic and leek and cook until the leek is tender (about 3 minutes). 5. Cover, reduce heat, and let simmer until chicken is cooked through. 6. Stir in the sugar, soy sauce, Mirin, and sesame seeds. Cook until everything is heated through. 7. Adjust the flavor with the salt and pepper, as needed. 8. Sprinkle with the chopped green onion and serve over rice or noodles.

Classic Kung Pao Chicken

Prep Time: 5 minutes | Cook Time: 22 minutes | Serves: 3-4

1 pound boneless skinless chicken breast, cut into bite-size pieces
1 tablespoon cornstarch
2 teaspoons vegetable oil
3 tablespoons green onions, chopped
2 cloves garlic, minced
½ teaspoon red pepper flakes, or to taste
½ teaspoon ginger, grated
½ teaspoon sesame oil
⅓ cup toasted peanuts

For the Sauce:
2 tablespoons rice wine vinegar
2 tablespoons soy sauce
2 teaspoons sugar

1. Toss the sauce ingredients in a bowl and set aside. 2. Toss the chicken in the cornstarch and coat well. 3. Heat the vegetable oil in a wok, skillet, or frying pan over medium heat. 4. Stir-fry the chicken until cooked through (about 7 minutes). Transfer the chicken to a plate. 5. Add the onions, garlic, red pepper flakes, red pepper flakes, and ginger to wok. Stir-fry until fragrant (about 30 seconds). 6. Stir in the sauce. 7. Return the chicken to the wok and stir to coat well with the sauce. 8. Add the nuts and continue cooking until all ingredients are cooked through and well coated with sauce. 9. Stir in the sesame oil. 10. Serve over rice.

Delicious Chicken with Onion and Scallions

Prep Time: 15 minutes | Cook Time: 5 minutes | Serves: 2

½ pound chicken breasts, boneless and skinless, sliced thinly
2 tablespoons cooking oil
½ onion, sliced
1 thumb ginger, peeled and sliced
For the Sauce:
2 teaspoons oyster sauce
1 tablespoon soy sauce
¼ teaspoon dark soy sauce
¼ teaspoon ground white pepper
3 stalks scallion, sliced
For the Marinade:
1 teaspoon cornstarch
1 teaspoon Chinese cooking wine
½ teaspoon sesame oil
1 tablespoon sugar
½ teaspoon cornstarch
3 tablespoons water

1. Combine the marinade ingredients. Add the chicken and let marinate for 10 minutes. 2. Stir together the sauce ingredients in a bowl. Set aside. 3. Heat 1 tablespoon oil in a wok, skillet, or frying pan over high heat. 4. Stir-fry the marinated chicken until lightly browned on the surface (about 3 minutes). Transfer to a plate. 5. Add the remaining oil to wok. 6. When the oil is hot, add the onion and ginger. 7. Stir-fry until fragrant (about 30 seconds). 8. Return the chicken to wok and stir-fry briefly. 9. Stir in the sauce. 10. Cook, with stirring, until chicken is cooked through. 11. Add the scallions. 12. Stir until all ingredients are coated with the sauce. 13. Serve with the rice.

Tasty Seared Chicken and Vegetables

Prep Time: 30 minutes | Cook Time: 10 minutes | Serves: 4

Coconut cream, one cup
Chicken stock, two cups
Minced garlic, one teaspoon
Minced ginger, one teaspoon
Brown sugar, two tablespoon
Shallot, one
Kaffir lime leaves, four
Lime wedges
Lemon grass, two sticks
Fish sauce, two tablespoon
Mix vegetables, one cup
Coconut milk, one cup
Cilantro, a quarter cup
Chicken pieces, half pound
Olive oil, one tablespoon

1. Take a large sauce wok. 2. Add the shallots and olive oil. 3. Cook your shallots and then add the chicken pieces. 4. When the chicken pieces are half cooked then add the chicken stock, minced garlic and ginger.5. Add the brown sugar and coconut milk. 6. Cook your ingredients until it starts boiling. 7. Add in the mixed vegetables, lemon grass and rest of the ingredients into your dish. 8. Cook your ingredients for ten minutes. 9. Add the coconut cream in the end and mix it for five minutes. 10. Garnish it with cilantro leaves. 11. Your dish is ready to be served.

Spicy Chicken and Vegetables Stir-Fry

Prep Time: 30 minutes | Cook Time: 10 minutes | Serves: 4

Red chili paste, one tablespoon
Mixed vegetables, two cups
Minced garlic, one teaspoon
Minced ginger, one teaspoon
Chopped onion, half cup
Chicken pieces, half pound
Minced ginger, half tablespoon
Lemon grass, two sticks
Fish sauce, two tablespoon
Chopped leeks, one cup
Coconut milk, one cup
Cilantro, a quarter cup
Olive oil, one tablespoon

1. Take a large sauce wok. 2. Add the chopped onion and olive oil. 3. Cook your chopped onion and then add the chicken. 4. Add the coconut milk. 5. Cook your ingredients until they start boiling. 6. Add in the chopped leeks, red chili paste and the rest of the ingredients. 7. Cook your ingredients for ten minutes. 8. Garnish it with cilantro leaves. 9. Your dish is ready to be served.

Salty Turkey and Asparagus Stir-Fry

Prep Time: 10 minutes | Cook Time: 20 minutes | Serves: 4

Fish sauce, two tablespoon
Soy sauce, half cup
Minced turkey meat, three cups
Tomatoes, two
Cilantro, half cup
Salt and pepper, to taste
Minced ginger, half tablespoon
Vegetable oil, two tablespoon
Red chili peppers, three
Chopped asparagus, one cup
Onion, one
Scallions, half cup
Minced garlic, one teaspoon

1. In a large wok, add the shallots and oil. 2. Cook your shallots and then add the ginger and garlic. 3. Cook the ginger and garlic and then add in the minced turkey meat. 4. Stir fry the turkey meat. 5. Add all the spices and the rest of the ingredients into your dish except the chopped asparagus. 6. When your turkey is cooked then, add the chopped asparagus. 7. Cook your dish for five minutes. 8. Garnish your dish with cilantro. 9. Your dish is ready to be served.

Cumin Black Pepper Chicken

Prep Time: 30 minutes | Cook Time: 20 minutes | Serves: 4

Minced garlic, two tablespoon
Minced ginger, two tablespoon
Cilantro, half cup
Olive oil, two tablespoon
Chopped tomatoes, one cup
Powdered cumin, one tablespoon
Salt, to taste
Black pepper, two tablespoon
Turmeric powder, one teaspoon
Onion, one cup
Vegetable broth, one cup
Smoked paprika, half teaspoon
Water, half cup
Chicken breast, one pound

1.Take a wok. 2. Add in the oil and onions. 3. Cook the onions until they become soft and fragrant. 4. Add in the chopped garlic and ginger. 5. Cook the mixture and add the tomatoes into it. 6. Add the spices. 7. When the tomatoes are done, add the chicken into it. 8. Mix the chicken so that the tomatoes and spices are coated all over the chicken. 9. Cook for five minutes. 10. Add in the water. 11. Mix the ingredients carefully and cover your wok. 12. When your chicken is done, add in the cilantro. 13. Mix your chicken and let it cook for an additional five minutes. 14. Your dish is ready to be served.

Classic Sweet and Sour Chicken

Prep Time: 30 minutes | Cook Time: 10 minutes | Serves: 4

Chives, one cup
Chicken stock, two cups
Minced garlic, one teaspoon
Minced ginger, one teaspoon
Chinese 5 spice, two tablespoon
Red onion, one
Kaffir lime leaves, four
Lime wedges
Lemon grass, two sticks
Fish sauce, two tablespoon
Mix vegetables, one cup
Cilantro, a quarter cup
Chicken pieces, half pound
Sweet and sour sauce, one cup
Olive oil, one tablespoon

1.Take a large sauce wok. 2. Add the shallots and olive oil. 3. Cook your shallots and then add the chicken pieces. 4. When the chicken pieces are half cooked then add the chicken stock, minced garlic and ginger. 5. Add the Chinese 5 spice and the rest of the spices. 6. Cook your ingredients until they start boiling. 7. Add in the mixed vegetables, lemon grass and rest of the ingredients into your dish. 8. Cook your ingredients for ten minutes. 9. Add the sweet and sour sauce and chives in the end and mix it for five minutes. 10. Garnish it with cilantro leaves. 11. Your dish is ready to be served.

Garlic Teriyaki Chicken Stir Fry with Noodles

Prep Time: 10 minutes | Cook Time: 20 minutes | Serves: 4

1 large skinless, boneless chicken breast, cut in bite-sized pieces
1 pinch garlic powder, or to taste
1 pinch onion powder, or to taste
freshly ground black pepper to taste
1 (8 oz) package dried rice noodles
4 C. hot water, or as needed
3 tbsp vegetable oil, divided
4 cloves garlic, minced
1 onion, chopped
1 green bell pepper, chopped
½ C. white cooking wine, or to taste
¼ C. soy sauce, or to taste
2 tbsp teriyaki sauce, or to taste
1 (6 oz) can sweet baby corn, drained
3 green onions, chopped

1. Season the chicken with the onion powder, garlic powder, and black pepper. 2. Fill a large bowl with the hot water. Place in it the noodles and let the soak for 12 min. Remove it from the water and slice it in half. 3. Place a large wok over medium heat. Heat 1½ tbsp of oil in it. Add the garlic and cook for 1 minute 30 sec. 4. Stir in the bell pepper with onion and cook them for 6 min while stirring all the time. Stir in the remaining oil. 5. Add the chicken and cook them for 8 min while stirring them often. Add the wine, soy sauce, and teriyaki sauce. Cook the stir fry for 4 min. 6. Stir in the baby corn and green onions with rice and noodles. Cook them for 4 min. 7. Serve your stir fry warm. Enjoy.

Grilled Chicken Stir Fry Linguine with Mushrooms

Prep Time: 10 minutes | Cook Time: 12 minutes | Serves: 6

1 (22 oz) package Tyson(R) Grilled and Ready(R) Fully Cooked Frozen Grilled Chicken Breast Strips
2 C. sliced fresh mushrooms
2 tbsp vegetable oil
2 C. frozen sweet pepper stir-fry
⅔ C. stir-fry sauce
1 lb linguine, prepared according to package directions

1. Cook the chicken according to the instructions on the package. 2. Place a large wok or wok over medium heat. Heat the oil in it. Add the mushroom and cook it for 5 min. 3. Stir in the pepper and cook them for 3 min. Stir in the chicken with sauce and cook them for 4 min. 4. Serve your stir fry hot with the linguine. Enjoy.

Tropical Chicken Stir Fry with Pepper

Prep Time: 10 minutes | Cook Time: 30 minutes | Serves: 6

¼ C. reduced-salt soy sauce
2 tbsp white wine vinegar
2 tbsp mirin (sweetened Asian wine)
1 tsp grated ginger root
2 crushed garlic cloves
1 tbsp cornstarch
2 tbsp oil, preferably sesame oil
1 lb boneless, skinless chicken breast, cut in 1-inch pieces
6 large green onions, cut in 1-inch pieces
2 C. fresh or frozen pepper strips
1 (20 oz) can chunk pineapple in juice
¼ C. sliced almonds (optional)

1. In a large mixing bowl: Whisk the soy sauce with the mirin, vinegar, ginger, cornstarch and garlic in it. 2. Place a large wok over medium heat. Heat the oil in it. Cook in it the chicken for 6 minutes. Drain it and place it aside. 3. Stir the green onions, peppers and pineapple to the wok and cook them for 4 min. 4. Stir in the back the chicken and cook them for another 4 min. 5. Serve your stir fry warm. Enjoy.

Lime Coconut Chicken Stir Fry

Prep Time: 15 minutes | Cook Time: 25 minutes | Serves: 4

1 ½ lb skinless, boneless chicken breast halves - cut into 1 inch cubes
2 limes, zested and juiced
2 tbsp grated fresh ginger root
1 ¾ C. coconut milk
½ tsp white sugar
1 C. jasmine rice
1 tbsp sesame oil
1 tbsp honey
¼ C. sweetened flaked coconut

1. In a large mixing bowl: Combine in it the chicken breast cubes with lime juice, lime zest, and grated ginger. Stir them. Place the mix aside for 22 min. 2. Place a small saucepan over medium heat. Stir in the coconut milk and sugar. Cook them until they start simmering. Add the rice. Lower the heat and cook them for 22 min. 3. Place a large wok over medium heat. Heat the oil in it. Stir in the chicken with marinade. Cook them for 4 min. 4. Add the honey and cook them for 2 min. Drain the rice and place it aside to cool down slightly. 5. Serve your honey chicken with rice and coconut flakes warm. Enjoy.

Orange Nutty Chicken and Carrot Stir Fry

Prep Time: 10 minutes | Cook Time: 20 minutes | Serves: 6

2 tsp peanut oil
2 stalks celery, chopped
2 carrots, peeled and diagonally sliced
1 ½ lb skinless, boneless chicken breast halves - cut into strips
1 tbsp cornstarch
¾ C. orange juice
3 tbsp light soy sauce
1 tbsp honey
1 tsp minced fresh ginger root
¼ C. cashews
¼ C. minced green onions

1. Place a large wok over medium heat. Heat 1 teaspoon of oil in it. 2. Cook in it the celery with carrot for 4 min. Stir in the remaining oil with chicken then cook them for 6 min. 3. In a large mixing bowl: Whisk in it the orange juice with cornstarch. Add the soy sauce, honey and ginger then whisk them to make the sauce. 4. Stir the sauce to the wok and cook them until the sauce becomes thick. Serve your chicken stir fry warm with some cashews and green onions. 5. Enjoy.

Pecan Chicken with Vegetables Stir Fry

Prep Time: 15 minutes | Cook Time: 20 minutes | Serves: 4

1 tbsp extra virgin olive oil
4 skinless, boneless chicken breast halves - cut into strips
1 C. julienned carrots
1 small onion, chopped
1 C. fresh sliced mushrooms
1 zucchini squash, peeled and cut into 1 inch rounds
2 yellow summer squash, peeled and sliced into 1 inch pieces
½ C. pecan halves
1 tsp coarse ground black pepper

1. Place a large wok over medium heat. Grease it with oil. Add the chicken and cook it for 4 min. 2. Stir in the onion with carrot. Cook them for 4 min. Stir in the mushrooms, zucchini, and squash then cook them for 6 to 8 min. 3. Season them with some salt and pepper then cook them for 4 min. Serve your stir fry warm. Enjoy.

Fresh Spinach and Chicken Stir Fry

Prep Time: 10 minutes | Cook Time: 35 minutes | Serves: 6

1 tbsp soy sauce
2 tbsp water
1 tbsp white sugar
2 lb skinless, boneless chicken breast halves, cut into small pieces
1 tbsp vegetable oil
5 green onions, sliced
3 cloves garlic, chopped
3 tbsp vegetable oil
2 (6 oz) bags fresh baby spinach leaves
1 C. thinly sliced fresh basil

1. Get large mixing bowl: Whisk in it the soy sauce, water, and sugar. Toss in it the chicken and place it aside for 35 minutes. 2. Place a large wok over medium heat. Heat 1 tbsp of oil in it. Cook in it the green onion with garlic for 2 min. Drain the mix and place it aside. 3. Heat 3 tbsp of oil in the same pan. Cook in it the chicken with marinade for 6 minutes. 4. Stir in the spinach and put on the lid. Cook them for 5 min while stirring them from time to time. 5. Add the cooked onion and garlic mix. Cook them for 3 min. Add the basil and cook them for another 3 min. Serve your stir fry warm. Enjoy.

Savory Canola Mushroom Chicken Stir Fry

Prep Time: 20 minutes | Cook Time: 15 minutes | Serves: 4

½ large eggplant, sliced into rounds
⅛ tsp salt
4 skinless, boneless chicken breast halves, cut into cubes
2 cloves garlic, minced
2 tbsp soy sauce
1 tbsp canola oil
2 C. mushrooms, sliced
⅛ tsp ground black pepper
4 C. spinach

1. Season the eggplant slices with some salt. Place them aside to rest for 6 minutes. Cut them into the dices. 2. Place a large wok over heat and grease it with some oil. Add with chicken, garlic, and soy sauce. Cook them for 12 min. 3. Add the mushroom with black pepper. Cook them for 4 min. 4. Place another wok over medium heat. Heat the canola oil in it. Cook the eggplant until it becomes golden brown. 5. Transfer the eggplant to the chicken stir fry with spinach and cook them for 4 min. Serve your stir fry warm. Enjoy.

Classic Tamari Veggies and Chicken Stir Fry

Prep Time: 15 minutes | Cook Time: 45 minutes | Serves: 4

1 (16 oz) package dry whole-wheat noodles
½ C. chicken stock
½ C. orange marmalade
⅓ C. tamari sauce
1 (1 inch) piece ginger root, peeled
ground black pepper to taste
1 lemon, juiced
3 tbsp peanut oil
2 lb skinless, boneless chicken breast halves, cut into thin strips
1 (16 oz) bag frozen stir-fry vegetables, thawed

1. Cook the noodles according to the directions on the package. Remove it from the water and place it aside. 2. Place a large saucepan over medium heat. Stir in it the stock, orange marmalade, tamari sauce, whole ginger root piece, and ground black pepper to make the sauce. 3. Cook them until they start boiling. Lower the heat and cook the sauce until it becomes thick for 22 min. 4. Turn off the heat and add the lemon juice. Place the sauce aside.
Place a large wok or wok over medium heat. Heat the oil in it. Cook in it the chicken for 8 min. Drain it and place it aside. 5. Add the veggies to the wok and cook them for 6 min. Discard the ginger root. Add the chicken back with sauce and stir them. Cook them for 3 min. 6. Serve your chicken stir fry with noodles warm. Enjoy.

Tasty Ramen Chicken Stir Fry

Prep Time: 15 minutes | Cook Time: 15 minutes | Serves: 8

3 tbsp vegetable oil
3 skinless, boneless chicken breast halves - cut into strips
2 stalks celery, chopped
2 zucchini, quartered and sliced
10 mushrooms, sliced
2 C. chopped spinach
1 (3 oz) package ramen noodle pasta with flavor packet
1 C. uncooked long-grain rice
1 tbsp cornstarch
¼ C. cold water
1 tsp vegetable oil
¼ C. soy sauce

1. Place a large wok over medium heat. Heat the oil in it. Cook in it the chicken for 8 min. 2. Add the celery with zucchini and cook them for 4 min. Stir in the spinach with mushroom and cook them for 3 min. 3. Lower the heat and keep them cooking while stirring from time to time. 4. Cook the rice and ramen noodles according to the instructions on the packages. Drain them and place them aside. 5. In a large mixing bowl: Whisk in it the cornstarch, water, oil and soy sauce. Stir the mix into the wok with the veggies. Add the noodles and rice then toss them to coat. 6. Cook them for 6 min. Serve your stir fry right away. Enjoy.

Chinese Chicken and Tofu Clash Stir Fry

Prep Time: 15 minutes | Cook Time: 15 minutes | Serves: 6

3 tbsp light soy sauce
1 tsp white sugar
1 tbsp cornstarch
3 tbsp Chinese rice wine
1 medium green onion, diced
2 skinless, boneless chicken breast halves - cut into bite-size pieces
3 cloves garlic, chopped
1 yellow onion, thinly sliced
2 green bell peppers, thinly sliced
1 (12 oz) package firm tofu, drained and cubed
½ C. water
2 tbsp oyster sauce
1 ½ tbsp chili paste with garlic

1. Get a mixing bowl: Combine in it the soy sauce, sugar, cornstarch, and rice wine. Whisk them well. Stir in the chicken with onion. Place them aside for 17 min. 2. Place a large wok over medium heat and grease it with oil. Cook in the chicken and onion with the marinade for 6 min. Add the garlic, onion, and peppers. Cook them for 6 min. Stir in the tofu, oyster sauce, water, and chili paste. 3. Cook them for 5 min while stirring often. 4. Serve your stir fry warm. Enjoy.

Sweet Pineapple and Apricot Chicken Stir Fry with Vegetables

Prep Time: 25 minutes | Cook Time: 15 minutes | Serves: 6

1 (15 oz) can apricot halves, drained and chopped, juice reserved
2 tbsp soy sauce
1 tbsp cornstarch
½ tsp garlic powder
½ tsp onion powder
½ tsp crushed red pepper flakes
2 tbsp vegetable oil
1 tbsp minced fresh ginger root
1 lb skinless, boneless chicken breast meat - cut into strips
1 (16 oz) package frozen stir-fry vegetables, thawed
1 (8 oz) can pineapple chunks, drained
3 green onion, sliced

1. Get a mixing bowl: Mix in it the apricot juice, soy sauce, cornstarch, onion powder, garlic powder, and red pepper flakes. Add the cornstarch and mix them well to make the sauce. 2. Place a large wok or wok over medium heat. Heat the oil in it. Add the ginger and cook it for 15 sec. Stir in the chicken and cook it for 8 min. 3. Add the veggies and cook for 6 to 8 minutes. Add the pineapple chunks, apricots, and sauce. Cook the stir fry for 2 min. 4. Fold in the green onion then serve it warm. Enjoy.

Hoisin Ginger Chicken Stir Fry

Prep Time: 15 minutes | Cook Time: 10 minutes | Serves: 4

3 skinless, boneless chicken breast halves
1 (2 inch) piece fresh ginger root
2 tbsp coconut oil
2 ½ tsp pressed garlic
⅓ C. hoisin sauce

1. Cut the chicken breasts into strips and place them aside. Remove the peel of the ginger root and grate it. 2. Place a large wok over medium heat. Heat the coconut oil in it. Add the garlic with ginger and cook them for 30 sec. 3. Stir in the chicken with hoisin sauce and cook them for 8 min. 4. Serve your stir fry warm. Enjoy.

Lemony Scallion Mushroom Chicken Stir Fry

Prep Time: 20 minutes | Cook Time: 20 minutes | Serves: 4

1 lemon
½ C. reduced sodium chicken broth
3 tbsp reduced-sodium soy sauce
2 tsp cornstarch
1 tbsp canola oil
1 lb boneless skinless chicken breasts, trimmed and cut into 1-inch pieces
10 oz mushrooms, halved or quartered
1 C. diagonally sliced carrots (¼-inch thick)
2 C. snow peas, stem and strings removed
1 bunch scallions, cut into 1-inch pieces, white and green parts divided
1 tbsp chopped garlic

1. Reserve 1 tbsp of grated lemon zest from the lemon. 2. Get a mixing bowl: Whisk 3 tbsp of the juice with the broth, soy sauce and cornstarch in it. 3. Place a wok or wok over medium heat. Heat the oil in it. Brown in it the chicken for 6 minutes. Drain it and place it aside. 4. Stir in the mushroom with the carrot and cook them for 6 minutes. Stir in the snow peas, garlic, scallion whites, and lemon zest. Cook them for 30 seconds. 5. Stir in the lemon juice mix and cook them for 4 min until the sauce becomes thick. Stir in the scallions with the cooked chicken. 6. Cook them for 3 min and then serve it warm. Enjoy.

Mayo Honey Chicken Stir Fry

Prep Time: 15 minutes | Cook Time: 15 minutes | Serves: 5

⅓ C. sweetened condensed milk
⅓ C. mayonnaise
1 tsp white sugar
2 tsp white vinegar
2 tsp honey
2 lb skinless, boneless chicken breast halves - diced
6 eggs, beaten
1 C. all-purpose flour
⅓ C. canola oil

1. In a large mixing bowl: Whisk the condensed milk, sugar, vinegar, mayonnaise, and honey to make the sauce in it. Place it aside. 2. In a large mixing bowl: Toss in it the chicken with eggs. Drain the chicken dices and dust them with the flour. 3. Place a large work or wok over medium heat. Heat the oil in it. Brown in it the chicken for 3 min. Add the sauce and cook them for 17 min until the chicken is cooked and the sauce is thick. 4. Serve your stir fry warm. Enjoy.

Spicy Mustard Chicken Stir Fry with Broccoli

Prep Time: 15 minutes | Cook Time: 30 minutes | Serves: 4

4 C. water
¼ tsp salt
2 tbsp butter
3 dried red chiles, broken into several pieces
2 C. uncooked white rice
1 tbsp sesame oil
2 garlic cloves, minced
2 tbsp soy sauce, divided
1 skinless, boneless chicken breast half, diced
1 tsp dried basil
1 tsp ground white pepper
½ tsp dry ground mustard
1 pinch ground turmeric
1 tbsp butter
1 ½ C. broccoli florets
1 C. diced green bell pepper
1 C. diced red bell pepper
½ C. diced onion
1 tsp lemon juice

1. Place a medium saucepan over medium heat. Stir in it the water, salt, 2 tbsp butter, and red chili peppers. Cook them until they start boiling. 2. Add the rice and put on lid. Cook it for 22 minutes over medium heat while stirring it from time to time. 3. Place a large wok over medium heat. Heat the oil in it. Cook in it the garlic for 2 minutes. 4. Stir in the half of the soy sauce with the chicken, basil, dry mustard, white pepper, and turmeric with garlic. Cook them for 9 minutes. Stir in the remaining soy sauce. 5. Place another wok or wok over medium heat. Heat 1 tbsp of butter in it. Cook in it the broccoli, red pepper, green pepper, and onion for 12 min. 6. Add the lemon juice and toss them. Stir the veggies into the chicken stir fry. 7. Serve them warm. Enjoy.

Popping Teriyaki Chicken Stir Fry with Vegetables

Prep Time: 10 minutes | Cook Time: 15 minutes | Serves: 4

2 tsp ground ginger
2 tbsp soy sauce
1 tsp rice vinegar
3 tbsp teriyaki sauce
2 tsp ground black pepper
2 tsp poppy seeds
2 tbsp sesame oil
2 cloves garlic, minced
½ large onion, quartered
2 skinless, boneless chicken breast halves, cut into 1-inch pieces
1 (16 oz) bag fresh stir-fry vegetables

1. Get a mixing bowl: Mix the ginger, black pepper, rice vinegar, soy sauce, teriyaki sauce, and poppy seeds to make the sauce in it. 2. Place a large wok over medium heat. Heat the oil in it. Add the onion with the garlic and cook them for 4 minutes. 3. Stir in the chicken and cook them for 6 minutes. Stir in the teriyaki sauce. Cook them until they start boiling. Add the veggies and cook them for 8 min. 4. Serve your stir fry right away with some white rice. Enjoy.

Classic Paprika Chicken with Vegetables

Prep Time: 25 minutes | Cook Time: 20 minutes | Serves: 4

1 tbsp flaked sea salt
2 tsp finely cracked black pepper
1 tsp crushed red pepper flakes, or to taste
1 tsp Chinese five-spice powder
1 tsp ground paprika
1 tbsp vegetable oil
4 skinless, boneless chicken breast halves -- trimmed and cut into quarters
1 lb broccoli florets, cut in half
3 small carrots, peeled and cut into matchstick-sized pieces

1. In a large mixing bowl: Combine in it the sea salt, red pepper flakes, black pepper, five-spice powder, and paprika. Mix them well. 2. Place a large wok over medium heat. Heat the oil in it. Massage the spice mix into the chicken and brown it for 12 min on each side. 3. Add the carrot with broccoli. Cook them for 14 min while stirring often. 4. Serve your stir fry warm. Enjoy.

Traditional Moo Goo Gai Pan

Prep Time: 5 minutes | Cook Time: 10 minutes | Serves: 2-4

¾ pound chicken breasts, boneless and skinless, sliced thinly
3 tablespoons vegetable oil, divided
1 cup fresh button mushrooms, sliced
½ cup canned bamboo shoots, rinsed and drained
½ cup canned water chestnuts, rinsed and drained
1 thumb ginger, chopped
1 clove garlic, minced

For the Marinade:
2 tablespoons soy sauce
1 tablespoon Chinese cooking wine
½ teaspoon sesame oil, or to taste
1 tablespoon cornstarch

For the Sauce:
½ cup chicken stock or broth
2 tablespoons oyster sauce
1 teaspoon sugar
1 tablespoon cornstarch

1. Combine the ingredients for marinade in a bowl with the chicken. Rub into chicken and let marinate for 15 minutes. 2. In a bowl, mix the sauce ingredients together and set aside. 3. Heat 2 tablespoons oil in a wok, skillet, or frying pan. 4. Add the chicken and stir-fry until browned on the surface (about 3–5 minutes). Transfer to a plate. 5. Add the remaining oil to wok and stir-fry ginger and garlic for about 30 seconds until fragrant. 6. Stir in the mushrooms and stir-fry for about 1 minute. 7. Add the bamboo shoots and water chestnuts, stir-frying to heat through. 8. Give the reserved sauce mixture a quick stir and pour into wok. 9. Cook, with stirring, until thickened. 10. Return the chicken to the wok and stir until well-coated and cooked through.

Classic Mongolian Chicken

Prep Time: 5 minutes | Cook Time: 15 minutes | Serves: 2-4

1 pound chicken breasts or thighs, skinless, boneless, cut into bite-size pieces
3 tablespoons vegetable oil, divided
½ small onion, chopped
2 cloves garlic, minced
1 medium bell pepper, sliced into strips
2 green onions, plus extra for garnish, chopped
½ teaspoon red pepper flakes, or to taste
1½ cups mung bean sprouts, blanched for 15 seconds and drained

For the Marinade:
2 tablespoons oyster sauce
½ teaspoon sugar
1 teaspoon cornstarch

For the Sauce:
4 teaspoons hoisin sauce
1 tablespoon dark soy sauce
2 teaspoons red wine vinegar
½ teaspoon sugar
2 tablespoons water

For the Thickener:
2 teaspoons cornstarch
4 teaspoons water

1. Combine the marinade ingredients. Add the chicken and allow to marinate for 15 minutes. 2. Stir together sauce ingredients in a bowl. Set aside. 3. Stir together ingredients for thickener in a small bowl or cup and set aside. 4. Heat the oil in a wok, skillet, or frying pan over high heat. 5. Stir-fry the marinated chicken until browned on the surface (about 5 minutes). Transfer to a plate. 6. Wipe pan clean and add remaining oil. 7. Add the onion, garlic, bell pepper, green onion, and hot pepper flakes. 8. Stir-fry until fragrant and tender (about 1 minute). 9. Return the chicken to wok and stir-fry to heat through (about 30 seconds). 10. Stir in the sauce. 11. Give thickener a quick stir and stir into wok. 12. Cook, with stirring, until thickened. 13. Stir to coat everything with sauce. 14. Stir in bean sprouts and cook until heated through (about 1 minute). 15. Garnish with the green onion and serve.

Garlic Chicken and Vegetables

Prep Time: 5 minutes | Cook Time: 15 minutes | Serves: 4

1½ tablespoons vegetable oil, divided
1 pound boneless skinless chicken breast, cut into bite-size pieces
Salt and pepper to taste
1 cup broccoli florets
1 cup mushrooms, halved
1 yellow bell pepper, sliced thinly
4 cloves garlic, minced

For the Sauce:

¾ cup chicken broth
1½ teaspoons sugar
1 tablespoon soy sauce
2 teaspoons sesame oil
2 teaspoons cornstarch

1. Stir sauce ingredients together in a bowl and set aside. 2. Heat 1 tablespoon oil in a wok, skillet, or frying pan over high heat. 3. Add the chicken and season with the pepper and salt. 4. Stir-fry until browned on the surface (about 7 minutes). Transfer to a plate. 5. Add remaining oil to wok and heat over medium high heat. 6. Add the broccoli, mushrooms, and bell pepper and stir-fry until tender (about 5 minutes). 7. Reduce heat to medium. 8. Add the garlic and cook until fragrant (about 30 seconds). 9. Return chicken to wok. 10. Give the prepared sauce mixture a quick stir and pour into wok. 11. Bring the sauce to a boil and allow to simmer until thickened (about 2 minutes). Season the flavor with more salt and pepper, if needed. 12. Serve hot.

Chinese Cashew Chicken

Prep Time: 5 minutes | Cook Time: 10 minutes | Serves: 3-4

1 pound boneless, skinless chicken breasts, cubed
3–4 tablespoons oil for stir-frying, divided
1 clove garlic, minced
1 tablespoon green onion, chopped
¼ cup roasted cashew nuts

For the Marinade:

1 tablespoon Chinese cooking wine
2 teaspoons freshly squeezed ginger juice
½ teaspoon salt
1 tablespoon cornstarch

For the Sauce:

2 tablespoons hoisin sauce
2 tablespoons dark soy sauce
2 tablespoons water
1 teaspoon granulated sugar

1. Combine the first 3 marinade ingredients and add chicken. Sprinkle with the cornstarch and rub to coat. Let marinate for 20 minutes. 2. Stir the sauce ingredients together in a bowl and set aside. 3. Heat 2 tablespoons oil in a wok, skillet, or frying pan over medium high heat. 4. Add the garlic and stir-fry until fragrant (about 30 seconds). 5. Add the chicken and stir-fry until browned on the outside (about 5–7 minutes). Transfer to a plate. 6. Add the remaining oil (about 1–2 tablespoons, or as needed) to wok. 7. Add the green onion and stir-fry until tender. 8. Return the chicken to wok and stir just to heat through. 9. Add the sauce ingredients to cook until thickened. 10. Add the cashews and stir until ingredients are well-coated with sauce. 11. Serve hot.

Chapter 4 Beef, Pork and Lamb

Delicious Steak and Brussels Sprouts

Prep Time: 25 minutes | Cook Time: 25 minutes | Serves: 4

½ pound flank or skirt steak, thinly sliced against the grain
Salt, to taste
4 scallions, whites chopped, greens sliced
4 tablespoons vegetable oil, divided
1 pound Brussels sprouts, halved
3 cloves garlic, sliced
2 tablespoons grated ginger
2 medium carrots, peeled, thinly sliced diagonally
1 jalapeño, sliced into rings

For the Sauce:
3 tablespoons oyster sauce
3 tablespoons reduced-sodium soy sauce
2 tablespoons rice vinegar
¼ cup water

1. Separate the green parts of onion and set aside for garnishing. 2. Season the beef with salt. Set aside. 3. Stir together sauce ingredients in a bowl. Set aside. 4. Swirl 2 tablespoons oil into a wok, skillet, or frying pan and heat over medium high heat. 5. Add Brussels sprouts and cook, with occasional stirring, until golden brown (about 4 minutes). Cover and cook until tender-crisp (about 3 minutes). Transfer to a plate. 6. Wipe pan clean and add 1 tablespoon oil. Heat until almost smoking. 7. Lay the steak in wok and let cook until underside is browned. Flip over and cook 30 seconds. Remove from wok and add to Brussels sprouts. 8. Heat the remaining oil in wok. 9. Add whites of scallion, garlic, and ginger. Cook until fragrant (30 seconds). 10. Add carrots and jalapeño. Stir-fry until slightly tender (about 2 minutes). 11. Return steak and Brussels sprouts to wok and pour in sauce. 12. Stir to coat ingredients and until sauce is thickened. 13. Garnish with the green onion and serve with rice.

Simple Beef Stir-fry with Broccoli

Prep Time: 15 minutes | Cook Time: 25 minutes | Serves: 4

2 cups vegetable stock
2 tablespoons soy sauce
4 garlic cloves, chopped
2 teaspoons chili powder
1 pound top sirloin beef, thinly sliced
3 cups broccoli, chopped into florets
1 cup cremini mushrooms, sliced
1 cup sugar snaps peas
4 green onions, sliced
1 tablespoon fresh ginger, peeled and sliced
2 tablespoons grapeseed oil

1. Prepare the marinade in a shallow dish or a re-sealable plastic bag such as a Zip-lock bag, Mix vegetable stock, soy sauce, and chili powder. If you desire more spices, add ½ teaspoon cayenne pepper. Toss the beef in the sauce and marinate for 10-15 minutes. 2. On high heat, add the oil to the wok and when hot, put in the ginger, broccoli, mushrooms, green onions, peas, and ¼ of the marinade, cook for about 3 minutes or until the broccoli softens. Add beef and remaining marinade and cook until beef is browned. 3. Serve hot.

Tasty Sesame Beef and Vegetable Stir-fry

Prep Time: 30 minutes | Cook Time: 20 minutes | Serves: 4

1 pound lean top sirloin beef, cut into strips
1 bunch asparagus, bottoms cut off and stalks halved
1 large handful of green beans, stemmed and cut in half
2 onions, diced
1 cup low sodium beef stock
2 tablespoons sesame seeds
3 teaspoons basil
2 tablespoons grapeseed oil
2 cups cooked brown or white rice

1. On high heat, warm the grapeseed oil in wok and cook the beef until brown. Remove from wok. 2. Put the beef stock in the wok and heat until boiling. Add the asparagus, green beans, and onions and cook until tender. 3. Add the beef, sesame seeds, basil, and brown rice and cook until everything has absorbed the vegetable stock. 4. Serve warm and enjoy!

Cashew Beef Stir-Fry with Broccoli

Prep Time: 15 minutes | Cook Time: 15 minutes | Serves: 4

2 cloves of garlic, crushed and minced
1.5 tablespoons lime juice
1 tablespoon, rice wine vinegar
½ teaspoon cayenne pepper
2 teaspoons soy sauce
2 sirloin steaks, about 1 pound each, cut into large strips
2 tablespoons sesame oil
2 onions, diced
2 bell peppers, sliced into thin strips
1 cup of broccoli, chopped into florets
½ cup cashews
2 tablespoons grapeseed oil

1. Mix garlic, lime juice, rice wine vinegar, cayenne pepper, and soy sauce. Set aside. 2. Brush the beef with the sesame oil. On high heat, add the grapeseed oil in the wok and when it is hot, fry the beef in two batches until it is browned and cooked. Remove from the wok and set aside. 3. Sauté onions until they are tender. Add peppers and broccoli and cook for 4 minutes. Add cashews and cook for 2 minutes. 4. Put the beef back in and cook until warm. Serve with rice if you desire.

Spicy Rice Noodles with Beef and Vegetables

Prep Time: 15 minutes | Cook Time: 15 minutes | Serves: 4

2 big bunches of rice noodles
1 pound beef top sirloin, cubed
1½ cups broccoli, chopped into florets
2 onions, diced
2 organic red peppers, sliced into strips
2 tablespoons soy sauce
4 tablespoons hoisin sauce
2 teaspoons dried basil
3 teaspoons lemon juice
2 tablespoons grapeseed oil

1. Cook the rice noodles according to package instructions, drain, and set aside. 2. Heat the oil on medium-high and cook the beef in 2 batches. Remove from the wok and set aside. 3. Sauté onions until tender then add the broccoli and red pepper. Turn the heat down to medium and cook for a few minutes. 4. Add the cooked rice noodles, beef, hoisin sauce, basil, and lemon juice. Stir until everything is warm and serve.

Sticky Beef Curry

Prep Time: 5 minutes | Cook Time: 12 minutes | Serves: 4

1 pound flank steak, sliced thinly against the grain
1 tablespoon oil
½ cup beef stock
1 tablespoon black bean paste
Salt and white pepper, to taste
For the Marinade:
2 tablespoons rice vinegar
2 tablespoons soy sauce
2 tablespoons Chinese curry powder
For the Thickener:
1 tablespoon cornstarch
2 tablespoons water

1. Combine marinade ingredients in a bowl with the beef. Rub over the beef slices and then let marinate, refrigerated, for 30 minutes. 2. Stir ingredients for thickener together in a small bowl. Set aside. 3. Heat oil in a wok, skillet, or frying pan over high heat. 4. Sear the beef slices. If needed, do this in batches to get crisp results. Transfer to a plate and set aside. 5. Add broth to the wok and scrape any brown bits. 6. Stir in black bean paste. 7. Give thickener a quick stir and stir into wok. Continue stirring until smooth. 8. Cook until thickened (about 1 minute) and then add beef. 9. Let simmer for 3 minutes. 10. Add salt and pepper to taste. 11. Serve over rice.

Garlic Sesame Beef

Prep Time: 5 minutes | Cook Time: 10 minutes | Serves: 4

1 pound round steak, cut into strips
1–2 tablespoons cooking oil
For the Marinade:
¼ cup soy sauce
¼ cup white sugar
¼ cup vegetable oil
2 tablespoons sesame seeds
Green onion, chopped, for sprinkling (optional)

2 cloves garlic, minced
2 green onions, chopped

1. Combine ingredients for marinade in a bowl or Ziploc bag. 2. Marinate the beef, refrigerated, for 30 minutes to overnight. 3. Heat oil in a wok, skillet, or frying pan over medium high heat. 4. Add the marinated beef and stir-fry until evenly browned and cooked through (about 5 minutes). 5. Add the sesame seeds and cook for a couple of minutes more. 6. Sprinkle with the chopped green onion (if using) and serve over rice.

Beef and Tomato Stir-Fry

Prep Time: 10 minutes | Cook Time: 20 minutes | Serves: 4

Fish sauce, two tablespoon
Soy sauce, half cup
Beef pieces, three cups
Tomatoes, two
Cilantro, half cup
Salt and pepper, to taste
Minced ginger, half tablespoon
Vegetable oil, two tablespoon
Thai chili peppers, three
Toasted nuts, half cup
Onion, one
Scallions, half cup
Minced garlic, one teaspoon

1. In a large wok, add the shallots and oil. 2. Cook your shallots and then add the ginger and garlic. 3. Cook your ginger and garlic and then add in the beef pieces. 4. Stir fry your beef pieces well. 5. Add all the spices and the rest of the ingredients into your dish except the toasted nuts. 6. When your beef is cooked then add the toasted nuts. 7. Cook your dish for five minutes. 8. Garnish your dish with cilantro. 9. Your dish is ready to be served.

Delicious Shredded Pork with Crispy Tofu

Prep Time: 30 minutes | Cook Time: 10 minutes | Serves: 4

Mixed vegetables, one cup
Vegetable stock, two cups
Shaoxing wine, half cup
Shredded pork, half pound
Minced garlic, one teaspoon
Brown sugar, two tablespoon
Shallot, one
Kaffir lime leaves, four
Lime wedges
Lemon grass, two sticks
Fish sauce, two tablespoon
Thai red curry paste, two tablespoon
Coconut milk, one cup
Cilantro, a quarter cup
Tofu cubes, half pound
Sesame oil, one tablespoon
Olive oil, one tablespoon

1. Take a large sauce wok. 2. Add the shallots and olive oil. 3. Cook your shallots and then add the mixed vegetables. 4. When the mixed vegetables are half cooked, add the shredded pork, red curry paste, chicken stock, and minced garlic. 5. Add the curry leaves and coconut milk. 6. Cook your ingredients until they start boiling. 7. Add in the Shaoxing wine and rest of the ingredients into the dish. 8. In a separate wok, add the sesame oil and tofu cubes. 9. Cook your tofu cubes until they turn crispy. 10. Add the tofu cubes into your dish. 11. Cook your ingredients for ten minutes. 12. When your dish is cooked, dish it out. 13. Garnish it with cilantro leaves. 14. Your dish is ready to be served.

Traditional Mongolian Beef and Broccoli

Prep Time: 10 minutes | Cook Time: 20 minutes | Serves: 4

Fish sauce, two tablespoon
Soy sauce, half cup
Mongolian spice mix, two tablespoon
Beef pieces, three cups
Tomatoes, two
Broccoli florets, two cups
Cilantro, half cup
Salt and pepper, to taste
Minced ginger, half tablespoon
Vegetable oil, two tablespoon
Red chili peppers, three
Toasted nuts, half cup
Onion, one
Scallions, half cup
Minced garlic, one teaspoon

1. In a large wok, add the shallots and oil. 2. Cook your shallots and then add the ginger and garlic. 3. Cook your ginger and garlic and then add in the beef pieces. 4. Stir fry your beef pieces well. 5. Add the Mongolian spice mix and the rest of the ingredients into your dish except the toasted nuts. 6. When your beef is cooked then add the broccoli florets. 7. Cook your dish for five minutes. 8. Add the toasted nuts two minutes before switching off your stove. 9. Garnish your dish with cilantro. 10. Your dish is ready to be served.

Healthy Beef and Mushroom Stew

Prep Time: 30 minutes | Cook Time: 10 minutes | Serves: 4

Red sauce, half cup
Beef stock, two cups
Minced garlic, one teaspoon
Brown sugar, two tablespoon
Shallot, one
Ginger pieces, a quarter cup
Beef pieces, half pound
Kaffir lime leaves, four
Lemon grass, two sticks
Fish sauce, two tablespoon
Wild mushroom, one cup
Coconut milk, one cup
Cilantro, a quarter cup
Beef chunks, half pound
Olive oil, one tablespoon

1. Take a large sauce wok. 2. Add the shallots and olive oil. 3. Cook your shallots and then add the beef chunks. 4. When the beef chunks are cooked then add the red sauce, beef stock, and minced garlic. 5. Add the ginger pieces and coconut milk. 6. Cook your ingredients until they start boiling. 7. Add in the mushrooms and rest of the ingredients into your stew. 8. Cook your ingredients for ten minutes. 9. When your mushrooms are cooked, dish out your stew. 10. Garnish it with cilantro leaves. 11. Your dish is ready to be served.

Orange Tomato and Beef Stir-Fry

Prep Time: 10 minutes | Cook Time: 20 minutes | Serves: 4

Shredded orange peel, two tablespoon
Soy sauce, half cup
Beef meat, one pound
Tomatoes, two
Cilantro, half cup
Salt and pepper, to taste
Minced ginger, half tablespoon
Vegetable oil, two tablespoon
Red chili peppers, three
Orange juice, one cup
Onion, one
Scallions, half cup
Minced garlic, one teaspoon

1. In a large wok, add the shallots and oil. 2. Cook your shallots and then add the ginger and garlic. 3. Cook your ginger and garlic and then add in the beef meat. 4. Stir fry your beef meat. 5. Add all the spices and the rest of the ingredients into your dish except the orange juice and shredded orange peels. 6. When your beef is cooked, add the orange juice and shredded orange peel. 7. Cook your dish for five minutes. 8. Garnish your dish with cilantro. 9. Your dish is ready to be served.

American Ground Beef Ramen with Beans and Corn

Prep Time: 7 minutes | Cook Time: 18 minutes | Serves: 4

1 lb ground beef, drained
3 (3 oz.) packets beef-flavor ramen noodles
5 C. boiling water
¼-½ C. water
1 (16 oz.) cans corn
1 (16 oz.) cans peas
¼ C. soy sauce
½ tsp ground red pepper
1 dash cinnamon
2 tsp sugar

1. Place a large wok over medium heat. Heat a splash of oil in it. Add the beef and cook it for 8 min. Place it aside.
Place a large saucepan over medium heat. Heat 5 C. of water in it until it starts boiling. Cook in it the noodles for 3 to 4 min. 2. Remove the noodles from the water and stir it into the wok with the beef. 3. Add the water, corn, peas, soy sauce, red pepper, cinnamon, sugar and 1 and a half of the seasoning packets. Toss them to coat. 4. Let them cook for 6 min while stirring often. Serve your ramen Wok Hot. Enjoy.

Ginger Beef Ramen with Vegetables

Prep Time: 20 minutes | Cook Time: 40 minutes | Serves: 4

14 oz. dried ramen noodles
12 oz. beef sirloin, half frozen to make slicing easier
1 ½ quarts chicken stock
1 inch piece gingerroot, roughly sliced
2 garlic cloves, halved
2 tbsp sake
3 tbsp shoyu, plus
1 tbsp shoyu, for stir-frying
1 bok choy, trimmed and thinly shredded
2 tbsp peanut oil
8 dried shiitake mushrooms, soaked in warm water for 30 minutes, drained and thinly sliced
sea salt, to taste
fresh ground black pepper, to taste

1. Prepare the noodles according to the instructions on the package. Discard the water and place the noodles aside. Slice the beef into thin slices. 2. Place a large saucepan over medium heat. Heat the stock in it. Stir in it the ginger with the garlic and cook for 12 minutes over low heat. 3. Once the time is up, drain the ginger with garlic and discard them. Add the shoyu, sake, and salt and pepper to the broth. 4. Place a large wok over medium heat. Heat 1 tbsp of oil in it. Sauté in it the baby bok choy for 3 min. Drain it and place it aside. 5. Heat the remaining oil in the same wok. Sauté the beef with the mushroom for 4 minutes in it. Stir into them the shoyu with a pinch of salt and pepper. 6. Stir the noodles in some hot water to heat it and then drain it. Place it in serving bowls and then top it with the beef, shiitake, and bok choy. 7. Pour the chicken broth all over them. Serve it right away. Enjoy.

Garlic Ramen Steak with Vegetables

Prep Time: 10 minutes | Cook Time: 15 minutes | Serves: 4

1 lb beef round tip steak, stripped
2 cloves garlic, minced
1 tbsp light sesame oil
¼ tsp ground red pepper
1 (3 oz.) packages ramen noodles
1 (1 lb) package broccoli, carrots and water chestnuts
1 tsp light sesame oil
1 (4 ½ oz.) jars mushrooms, drained
1 tbsp soy sauce

1. Get a mixing bowl: Stir in it the beef strips, garlic, one tbsp sesame oil and ground red pepper. 2. Place a pot over medium heat. Cook in it 2 C. of water until it starts boiling. Crush the noodles into 3 portions. 3. Stir it in the pot with the veggies and cook them until they start boiling. Lower the heat and cook them for an extra 3 min. 4.Pour the mix in a colander to remove the water. Place the noodles and veggies mix back into the pot. 5. Add the seasoning packet and stir them well. 6. Place a large wok over medium heat. Heat 1 tsp of sesame oil in it. Cook the beef slices for 4 to 5 minutes in it or until they are done. 7. Stir the ramen and veggies mix into the wok with the mushrooms and soy sauce. Cook them for an extra 3 min. 8. Serve your wok warm. Enjoy.

Beef and Vegetables Stir-Fry

Prep Time: 30 minutes | Cook Time: 15 minutes | Serves: 8

2 pounds boneless beef sirloin or beef top round steaks (¾" thick)
3 tbsps cornstarch
1 (10.5 ounce) can Campbell's® Condensed Beef Broth
½ cup soy sauce
2 tbsps sugar
2 tbsps vegetable oil
4 cups sliced shiitake mushrooms
1 head Chinese cabbage (bok choy), thinly sliced
2 medium red peppers, cut into 2"-long strips
3 stalks celery, sliced
2 medium green onions, cut into 2" pieces
Hot cooked regular long-grain white rice

1. To start this recipe grab a knife and begin to cut your beef into some thin long strips. 2. In a medium sized bowl and combine the following ingredients: sugar, broth, soy, and cornstarch. 3. After combining the ingredients set them aside. 4. Get your wok hot over a high level of heat and add one 1 tbsp of oil to it. 5. Once your oil is hot combine the following ingredients in it: green onions, mushrooms, celery, cabbage, and peppers. 6. Fry these veggies down until you find that they are soft. Set aside. 7. Now grab your cornstarch mixture and put it in the pot. Stir-fry until you find that it has thickened. 8. Once thick, combine the cornstarch with your beef and veggies. 9. Fry until beef is cooked completely. 10. Let contents cool. Enjoy.

Delicious Chinese-Style Braised Beef Stew

Prep Time: 15 minutes | Cook Time: 3 hours | Serves: 8

2 tablespoons vegetable oil
3 pounds beef rough flank, cut into 1½-inch to 2-inch pieces
7 ginger slices
3 pieces star anise
1 cup Shaoxing wine
1 tablespoon dark soy sauce
5 cups water
2 pounds daikon radish, chopped
3 scallions, cut into 2-inch pieces
5 cloves
3 bay leaves
3 tablespoons light soy sauce
1 tablespoon oyster sauce
1 tablespoon sugar
Salt, to taste
1 tablespoon cornstarch plus 2 tablespoons water

1. Place the steak in a big pot with enough water to cover it. 2. Bring to a boil over high heat and then cook the beef for 1 minute. 3. Remove the beef pieces from the heat, drain, and thoroughly rinse them. 4. In a wok over medium heat, put the oil, add the cloves, ginger, bay leaves, and star anise. 5. Increase the heat to high and cook for 3 minutes, or until aromatic.
Return the meat to the wok and simmer for another 10 minutes, or until the edges are lightly browned. 6. Bring to a boil with the light soy sauce, Shaoxing wine, dark soy sauce, and oyster sauce. 7. Add the water and sugar and bring it back to a boil. 8. Reduce the heat to medium-low, cover, and cook for 2 hours, stirring periodically. 9. Gently toss in the daikon and cook for an additional 45 minutes, or until the daikon is soft. 10. Add the scallions and season with the salt. 11. Mix the cornstarch and 2 tablespoons of water to make a slurry. 12. Decant the slurry into the sauce and stir until it slightly thickens.

Tasty Tipsy Japanese Crumbled Beef

Prep Time: 10 minutes | Cook Time: 6 minutes | Serves: 4

¾ lb ground beef
2 tbsp freshly grated ginger
3 tbsp soy sauce
3 tbsp sake
2 tbsp mirin
1 tbsp white sugar, or more to taste

1. Place a large wok over medium heat and heat it. Add the beef and cook for 8 minutes. 2. Stir in the remaining ingredients. Cook them until they start boiling. Keep boiling them for 2 min. 3. Serve your crumbled beef warm with some rice. Enjoy.

Homemade Mung Bang Noodles Wok

Prep Time: 30 minutes | Cook Time: 17 minutes | Serves: 6

1 lb lean ground beef, cooked
6 slices turkey bacon, chopped
2 (3 oz.) packages ramen noodles
3 garlic cloves, minced
1 medium red onion, diced
1 medium cabbage, chopped
3 carrots, cut into thin 1 inch strips
1 red bell pepper, cut into bite size pieces
2-4 tbsp light soy sauce
3 C. bean sprouts
Light soy sauce, to taste
Crushed red pepper flakes

1. Place a large wok over medium heat. 2. Cook the bacon in it until it becomes crisp. Drain it and place it aside. Keep about 2 tbsp of the bacon grease in the pan. 3. Sauté the garlic with onion for 4 minutes in it. Stir in 2 tbsp of soy sauce and the carrots. 4. Let cook for 3 minutes. Stir in the bell pepper with the cabbage and let cook for an extra 7 minutes. 5. Cook the noodles according to the manufacturer's directions. Drain it and stir it with a splash of olive oil. 6. Stir the beef, bacon, and crushed red pepper flakes into the wok with the cooked veggies. Let cook for 4 minutes while stirring often. 7. Once the time is up, stir the bean sprouts and Ramen noodles into the veggies mix. Let cook for an extra 3 minutes while stirring all the time. 8. Serve the noodles wok warm with some hot sauce. Enjoy.

Chinese-Style Tofu with Ground Pork

Prep Time: 10 minutes | Cook Time: 10 minutes | Serves: 4

2 tablespoons soy sauce
2 tablespoons rice wine
1 tablespoon cornstarch
2 tablespoons cooking oil
½ pound extra-firm tofu, cut into 1-inch cubes
1 medium carrot, roll-cut into ½-inch pieces
1 tablespoon crushed, chopped ginger
4 garlic cloves, crushed and chopped
½ pound ground pork
1 medium onion, cut into 1-inch pieces
1 teaspoon Chinese five-spice powder
1 medium red bell pepper, cut into 1-inch pieces
4 scallions, cut into 1-inch pieces

1. In a small bowl, stir together the rice wine, soy sauce, and cornstarch. Set aside. 2. In a wok over high heat, heat the cooking oil until it shimmers. 3. Add the tofu, carrot, ginger, and garlic and stir-fry for 4 minutes. 4. Add the pork, onion, and five-spice powder and stir-fry for 4 minutes. 5. Add the bell pepper and cook for 2 minutes. 6. Place in the soy sauce mixture and stir until a glaze forms. 7. Garnish with the scallions and serve.

Classic Mongolian Beef in Soy Sauce

Prep Time: 15 minutes | Cook Time: 10 minutes | Serves: 3

1 teaspoon vegetable oil plus ⅓ cup, for frying
8 ounces flank steak, sliced against the grain
1 teaspoon soy sauce
2 tablespoons brown sugar
¼ cup low-sodium soy sauce
5 dried red chili peppers
1 tablespoon cornstarch plus 2 tablespoons water
1 tablespoon cornstarch plus ¼ cup, divided
¼ cup low-sodium chicken stock
½ teaspoon ginger, minced
2 cloves garlic, chopped
2 scallions

1. Toss the cut beef with1 teaspoon soy sauce, 1 tablespoon cornstarch, and 1 teaspoon oil. Allow for 1 hour of marinating. 2. Using the remaining ¼ cup of cornstarch, gently coat the marinated beef slices. 3. Stir together the ¼ cup low-sodium soy sauce, brown sugar, and chicken stock in a small bowl. 4. In a wok on high heat, heat ⅓ cup vegetable oil and add the flank steak pieces. 5. Cook for 1 minute and 30 seconds, flipping once. 6. Transfer to a sheet pan. 7. Remove all but 1 tablespoon of the oil from the wok and increase the heat to medium-high. 8. Stir in the dried chili peppers, ginger, and garlic. 9. Add the premixed sauce and stir for another 10 seconds. 10. Simmer the sauce for 2 minutes before slowly stirring in the cornstarch slurry mixture. 11. Add the beef and scallions after the sauce has thickened. 12. Toss everything together for 30 seconds more before serving.

Lamb and Sausage Stew with Carrots and Potatoes

Prep Time: 20 minutes | Cook Time: 2 hours | Serves: 6

½ pound spicy Italian sausage
2 tablespoons olive oil, divided
1½ pounds boneless leg of lamb, cut into 1½-inch pieces
¼ cup all-purpose flour
6 cloves garlic, smashed
1 cup red wine
2 large carrots, cut into large chunks
1 pound baby portabella mushrooms, quartered
¼ cup parsley, chopped
Salt and black pepper, to taste
1 large yellow onion, diced
2½ cups beef broth
15 ounces canned tomato sauce
1 pound Yukon gold potatoes, cut into large chunks
6 sprigs thyme

1. In a wok, heat 1 tablespoon of olive oil over medium-high heat. 2. Eliminate the sausage casings and cook the sausage in the oil until browned. Remove, place on a plate, and set aside. 3. Season the lamb pieces with the salt and pepper and toss with ¼ cup of all-purpose flour. 4. Shake off any extra flour from the lamb and place it in the wok. 5. Sear the lamb on all sides until each side is browned. Remove from the wok and set aside. 6. In the same wok, add the garlic cloves and onion. 7. Season the onions and garlic with salt and pepper, and cook for 5 minutes, or until the onions turn translucent. 8. Cook for another minute after adding the remaining flour. 9. Place in the broth and wine and bring to a gentle simmer. 10. Add the carrots, tomato sauce, mushrooms, potatoes, and thyme to the wok with the cooked lamb and sausage. 11. Season with salt and pepper to taste. Bring to a gentle simmer, cover, and reduce the heat. 12. Cook for 1 hour and 30 minutes and then top with the chopped parsley.

Simple and Tasty Chop Suey

Prep Time: 10 minutes | Cook Time: 30 minutes | Serves: 2

1 pound pork loin
1 carrot
½ cup basmati rice
1 tablespoon coconut oil
2 tablespoons soy sauce
½ teaspoon chili flakes
1 teaspoon sesame seeds
Salt and pepper, to taste

1. Wash the vegetables carefully and cut them into bite-sized pieces. 2. Rinse the meat under warm water, pat dry, and, if necessary, remove the tendons, then cut the pork into even cubes. Heat the wok and melt some coconut oil in it. 3. At the same time, cook the rice in a rice cooker or a saucepan with salted water. 4. Add the spices. 5. Add the meat and mix everything well. 6. When the meat has gained color, add the vegetables and sear everything for 5 minutes. Then deglaze everything with the soy sauce and simmer for a few minutes. 7. Mix with the rice before serving and season with salt and pepper. 8. Serve.

Refreshing Pork Stir Fry Pineapple and Peppers

Prep Time: 10 minutes | Cook Time: 12 minutes | Serves: 4

1 (8 ounces) can pineapple chunks, drained, juice reserved
¼ cup rice vinegar
2 tablespoons brown sugar
2 tablespoons cornstarch
2 tablespoons cooking oil
1 tablespoon crushed, chopped ginger
2 garlic cloves, crushed and chopped
1 pound pork tenderloin, cut into 1-inch pieces
2 chilies, cut into ¼-inch circles (no need to remove seeds or core)
1 medium onion, cut into 1-inch pieces
1 teaspoon hot sesame oil
4 scallions, cut into 1-inch pieces

1. Whisk together the rice vinegar, pineapple juice, brown sugar, and cornstarch in a small bowl. Set aside. 2. In a wok over high heat, heat the cooking oil until it shimmers. 3. Add the ginger, garlic, and pork and stir-fry for 7 minutes. 4. Add the chilies and onion and stir-fry for 3 minutes. 5. Add the pineapple chunks and sesame oil and stir-fry for 2 minutes. 6. Add the pineapple juice mixture and stir until a glaze forms. 7. Garnish with the scallions and serve.

Flavorful Stir-Fired Beef and Onion

Prep Time: 25 minutes | Cook Time: 5 minutes | Serves: 4

For the Beef and Marinade:

1-pound flank steak, thinly sliced against the grain
¼ teaspoon baking soda
1 teaspoon cornstarch
1 teaspoon canola oil
1 teaspoon oyster sauce
1 tablespoon water

For the Rest of the dish:

1 tablespoon light soy sauce
1 teaspoon dark soy sauce
2 teaspoons ketchup
¼ cup water
2 teaspoons oyster sauce
2 tablespoons oil
¼ teaspoon sugar
10 ounces small onions
¼ teaspoon sesame oil

1. Combine the flank steak, cornstarch, oil, oyster sauce, baking soda, and water in a medium mixing bowl. Refrigerate for up to 30 minutes. 2. Meanwhile, whisk together the dark soy sauce, light soy sauce, ketchup, sugar, sesame oil, oyster sauce, and water in a small mixing bowl. 3. Heat 1 tablespoon of oil in a wok over high heat until it smokes. 4. Arrange the beef in a single layer in the wok and cook for 1 minute, stirring occasionally, until browned. 5. Continue to stir-fry for another 30 seconds, or until the meat is about 75 percent done. 6. Add the onions and another tablespoon of oil to the wok. 7. Stir-fry for 90 seconds, or until the onions are browned and slightly blistered. 8. Remove the beef from the wok and add the prepared sauce to the wok, bringing it to a low simmer. 9. Cook for 15 seconds before adding the beef and onions and cooking for another 30 seconds. 10. Serve.

Traditional Pork Adobo

Prep Time: 5 minutes | Cook Time: 1 hour 45 minutes | Serves: 6

2 pounds pork shoulder, cut into chunks
2 tablespoons vegetable oil
¼ cup cane vinegar or white vinegar
6 garlic cloves, chopped
2 teaspoons black peppercorns
2 cups water
⅓ cup low-sodium soy sauce
1 bay leaf
2 teaspoons sugar

1. Heat the oil on medium-high heat in a wok and sear the pork until it's browned on all sides. 2. Bring the water, soy sauce, vinegar, garlic, peppercorns, bay leaf, and sugar to a boil. 3. Switch the heat to medium-low, cover, and cook for 1 hour. 4. Remove the lid and continue to reduce the sauce for another 30 minutes.

Easy Chinese Sausage and Snow Peas

Prep Time: 10 minutes | Cook Time: 5 minutes | Serves: 4

3 thin slices ginger
2 tablespoons oil
3 garlic cloves, thinly sliced
½ medium onion, sliced
1 tablespoon Shaoxing wine
½ teaspoon sesame oil
2 links Chinese sausage, thinly sliced
8 ounces snow peas
¼ teaspoon white pepper
¼ teaspoon salt

1. Add the ginger slices to 2 tablespoons of oil in a wok over medium-low heat and cook them for 20 seconds. 2. Add the garlic and Chinese sausage. Increase the heat to medium, and cook for 2 minutes. 3. Add the onions and snow peas. Mix everything well. 4. Add the white pepper, Shaoxing wine, sesame oil, and salt. Stir-fry everything for 2 more minutes. 5. Dish out to serve hot.

Crispy Pork Schnitzel

Prep Time: 35 minutes | Cook Time: 10 minutes | Serves: 4

4 pork loin chops, bone-in, center-cut, and pounded thoroughly
½ cup flour
2 large eggs, beaten
2½ cups unseasoned dried breadcrumbs
2 lemons, for marinating and for serving
1 teaspoon salt
½ cup frying oil
6 tablespoons butter

1. Put the egg, flour, and breadcrumbs in three separate shallow bowls. 2. Squeeze the lemon juice evenly and generously over both sides of the pork chops and then season evenly with salt. 3. Melt the butter and oil in the wok over medium heat. 4. Dredge the pork chops in the flour before dipping them in the egg. Finish by applying the breadcrumbs all over the pork chops. 5. Fry the pork chops for about 3 minutes on each side. 6. Serve and enjoy!

Classic Xi' an Lamb Burgers

Prep Time: 30 minutes | Cook Time: 10 minutes | Serves: 4

1 teaspoon Sichuan peppercorns
1 tablespoon cumin seeds
½ teaspoon red chili flakes
1 teaspoon salt
1 jalapeno, de-seeded and thinly sliced
1 tablespoon vegetable oil
2 cloves garlic, minced
1 cucumber, de-seeded and diced
1 pound ground lamb
1 medium red onion, thinly sliced
1 small red bell pepper, de-seeded and thinly sliced
1 cup plain Greek Yogurt
4 Brioche buns
1 cup fresh cilantro

1. Toast the Sichuan peppercorns, cumin seeds, and red chili flakes in a dry pan. Place them in a spice grinder and grind to a coarse powder. 2. Merge half of the spice mixture with the lamb and shape into four patties. Season each burger with salt. 3. Put the oil over high heat in a wok and sear the burgers on both sides until crisp, about 2 minutes per side. 4. Place them on a plate and cover with foil. 5. Put the onion and peppers with a little vegetable oil in the wok and cook until caramelized. 6. Finish by sprinkling the remaining spice mixture on top. 7. Combine the yogurt and garlic in a mixing bowl and season with the salt. 8. To assemble the burgers, place some of the yogurt mixture on the bottom of each bun and top with the diced cucumbers. 9. Add the burger, onion-pepper mixture, yogurt, and fresh cilantro on top.

Flavorful Sweet and Sour Pork

Prep Time: 10 minutes | Cook Time: 12 minutes | Serves: 4

1 (8 ounces) can pineapple chunks, drained, juice reserved
¼ cup rice vinegar
¼ cup plus 2 tablespoons cornstarch, divided
2 tablespoons brown sugar
1 pound pork tenderloin, cut into 1-inch pieces
¼ cup cooking oil
1 tablespoon crushed, chopped ginger
2 garlic cloves, crushed and chopped
1 medium red onion, cut into 1-inch pieces
1 red bell pepper, cut into 1-inch pieces
4 scallions, cut into 1-inch pieces

1. Whisk together the reserved pineapple juice, rice vinegar, two tablespoons of cornstarch, and brown sugar in a small bowl. Set aside. 2. Add the pork to a resealable plastic bag or covered bowl. Toss with the remaining ¼ cup of cornstarch to coat thoroughly. 3. In a wok over high heat, heat the cooking oil until it shimmers. 4. Add the ginger and garlic and stir-fry for 1 minute. 5. Add the pork and shallow-fry until lightly browned. Remove the pork and set it aside. 6. Remove and discard all but two tablespoons of oil from the wok. 7. Add the onion to the wok and cook for 1 minute. 8. Add the bell pepper and pineapple chunks and stir-fry for 1 minute. 9. Add the pineapple juice mixture and stir until a glaze forms. Stir in the cooked pork. 10. Garnish with the scallions and serve.

Scallion Beef and Romaine

Prep Time: 10 minutes | Cook Time: 10 minutes | Serves: 4

1 pound boneless short ribs, sliced thinly across the grain
2 tablespoons vegetable oil, divided
6 scallions, ends trimmed, cut diagonally
2 tablespoons sliced ginger
1 head of romaine, cut into 2-inch pieces
Salt, to taste
Toasted peanuts or cashews, for sprinkling

For the Marinade:
1½ teaspoons cornstarch
½ teaspoon red pepper flakes
Pinch of salt
1 tablespoon soy sauce

For the Sauce:
2 tablespoons soy sauce
2 tablespoons seasoned rice vinegar
2 tablespoons Chinese rice wine

1. Combine marinade ingredients in a bowl, add beef and toss. 2. In a small bowl, stir sauce ingredients together. Set aside. 3. In a wok, skillet, or frying pan, heat 1 tablespoon oil to shimmering. 4. Add scallion and ginger. Stir-fry until browned (about 2 minutes). 5. Add romaine and a pinch of salt, tossing until leaves turn bright green (about 4 minutes). Transfer veggies to a plate, keeping wok hot. 6. Add remaining oil and adjust heat to high. 9. When oil is almost smoking, lay beef on wok and let cook until underside is browned (about 1 minute). 10. Flip beef over and cook for 1–2 minutes, or until evenly browned. 11. Stir in sauce and veggies. 12. Toss until sauce is thickened (about 30 seconds). 13. Remove from heat and season with more salt, if needed. 14. Sprinkle with toasted nuts and serve with rice.

Savory Beef Chow Fun

Prep Time: 10 minutes | Cook Time: 15 minutes | Serves: 2

1 pound fresh flat rice noodles, cut 1–2 inches wide
6 ounces beef sirloin, sliced thinly against the grain
2–3 tablespoons cooking oil
4 stalks green onion, green parts cut into 3-inch pieces, whites halved
1 inch fresh ginger, peeled and minced
6 ounces bean sprouts

For the Sauce:
1 tablespoon oyster sauce
2 tablespoons soy sauce
2 tablespoons dark soy sauce
1 teaspoon sugar
¼ teaspoon white pepper powder

For the Marinade:
2 teaspoons soy sauce
1 teaspoon dark soy sauce
1 teaspoon cornstarch

1. In a shallow container or Ziploc bag, combine marinade ingredients and beef slices. Let marinate for 30 minutes. 2. In a bowl, stir all sauce ingredients together. Set aside. 3. Swirl oil in wok, skillet, or frying pan and heat until almost smoking. 4. Lay beef slices over bottom and let cook until browned underneath (about 1 minute). 5. Stir to flip and let cook quickly (30 seconds). Transfer to a plate. 6. Remove any brown bits from wok and add another tablespoon of oil, if needed. Heat up again to almost smoking. 7. Stir in whites of onion and ginger. Cook briefly until fragrant (about 30 seconds). 8. Lay noodles over wok and stir-fry quickly (30 seconds). 9. Stir in sauce and cook another 30 seconds. 10. Return beef to wok, stir-frying for 10 seconds. 11. Add bean sprouts and green onion. 12. Stir to heat through and turn off heat. 13. Serve immediately.

Celery Beef with Tomatoes

Prep Time: 5 minutes | Cook Time: 7 minutes | Serves: 4

1 pound sirloin beef, sliced thinly against the grain
4 large tomatoes, each cut into 6 pieces
2 ribs celery, sliced diagonally
2 spring onions, sliced diagonally
1-inch piece ginger, peeled and sliced
1 clove garlic, minced
2½ tablespoons vegetable oil
2 teaspoons sugar
¼ teaspoon salt, plus more to taste
Black pepper, to taste

For the Marinade:

2 tablespoons oyster sauce
1 tablespoon light soy sauce
1 teaspoon sugar
2 teaspoons vegetable oil
1¼ teaspoons cornstarch

For the Thickener:

1 tablespoon cornstarch
2 tablespoons water

1. Mix together the ingredients for marinade and marinate beef for 15 minutes. 2. In a small bowl or cup, stir thickener ingredients together. Set aside. 3. Heat a wok over medium high heat and swirl in 2 tablespoons oil. Heat until oil shimmers. 4. Briefly stir-fry garlic to release aroma. 5. Lay beef over wok and let cook until browned underneath. 6. Flip and let cook briefly (30 seconds) and not completely cooked though. Transfer to a plate. 7. Scrape any brown bits from the wok and wipe clean. 8. Heat remaining oil in same wok. 9. Stir-fry ginger until fragrant. 10. Add the celery, tomato, sugar, and ¼ teaspoon salt. 11. Cover and bring to a boil. 12. Push contents of wok to the side. 13. Stir thickener and pour into wok, stirring continuously. 14. When sauce has thickened, return beef to wok. 15. Cook and stir until the beef is cooked through. 16. Adjust flavor with soy sauce, salt, or black pepper, according to taste. 17. Serve with rice.

Onion Beef Lo Mein

Prep Time: 5 minutes | Cook Time: 15 minutes | Serves: 1

2–4 ounces beef, sliced thinly into strips
2 tablespoons vegetable oil, divided
1 small onion, sliced
2 red or green banana peppers, cut into long pieces
4 garlic cloves, sliced
Salt and pepper, to taste
3–4 ounces Lo Mein noodles, cooked according to packaging instructions
Sesame seeds, for sprinkling

For the Marinade:

1 tablespoon soy sauce
1 tablespoon cooking wine

For the Sauce:

½ tablespoon oyster sauce
1 tablespoon dark soy sauce
1 tablespoon cooking wine
Pinch of sugar

1. Toss the beef in marinade ingredients. Set aside to marinate for 10 minutes. 2. Stir together the sauce ingredients in a bowl and set aside. 3. Heat 1 tablespoon oil in wok, skillet, or frying pan over medium heat. 4. Add beef and cook until no longer pink. Transfer to a plate. 5. Add remaining oil to wok and add onion. Sauté for 2 minutes. 6. Add peppers and garlic. 7. Stir-fry until vegetables are tender (about 3 minutes). 8. Return beef to wok and stir-fry for about 1 minute. 9. Add noodles and sauce. 10. Raise heat and stir-fry carefully but thoroughly (chopsticks are best for this). 11. Season with salt and pepper, as needed. 12. Stir-fry for 1 minute. 13. Sprinkle with the sesame seeds and serve.

Yummy Spicy Beef and Eggplant

Prep Time: 20 minutes | Cook Time: 10 minutes | Serves: 6

For the Marinade:

¼ cup beef stock
2 tablespoons hoisin sauce
2 tablespoons oyster sauce
½ teaspoon cayenne pepper, more if you like it spicier

Other ingredients:

1½ pound flank steak, thinly sliced
2 tablespoons, grapeseed oil
3 tablespoons, chopped garlic
4 green onions cut into 2-inch-long slivers
2 Asian eggplants (long and thin), sliced thinly
1 tablespoon fresh basil (or 1 teaspoon dry)
1 tablespoon fresh thyme (or 1 teaspoon dry)

1. Mix the stock, hoisin sauce, oyster sauce, and cayenne pepper for the marinade sauce. Dip the beef slices in the marinade and let rest in the refrigerator for at least 30 minutes up to one hour. The longer you let the beef marinate, the stronger the flavors are. 2. While marinating the beef, prepare the vegetables. 3. Turn your stove to medium-high and heat the wok with grapeseed oil. When the oil is hot, place in the garlic in first. Allow to brown, about 30 seconds. Add the vegetables and cook for 3-4 minutes or until cooked through. Remove from the wok and set aside. 4. Add the beef and the marinade sauce. Stir-fry the beef until browned and the sauce has thickened, about 3-5 minutes. Add the vegetables and herbs. mix well, and stir-fry until just warm through, about 1 minute. 5. Serve warm.

Nutritious Beef with Bamboo Shoots

Prep Time: 10 minutes | Cook Time: 10 minutes | Serves: 3-4

2½ tablespoons oil, divided
1 pound flank steak, sliced thinly against the grain
1 clove garlic, minced, divided
1 large green bell pepper, sliced into strips
¼ medium red bell pepper, sliced into strips (optional)
1 (8-ounce) can bamboo shoots, rinsed and drained
1–2 tablespoons water or broth, as needed
2 green onions, sliced

For the Marinade:

1 tablespoon light soy sauce
2 tablespoons Chinese rice wine
1 teaspoon brown sugar
Black pepper, to taste
2 teaspoons vegetable oil
2 teaspoons cornstarch

For the Sauce:

1½ tablespoons oyster sauce
1 tablespoon dark soy sauce
2 tablespoons water

1. Stir th marinade ingredients together. Add beef strips and let marinate for 25 minutes. 2. Combine the sauce ingredients in a bowl. Set aside. 3. Heat 2 tablespoons oil in a preheated wok, skillet, or frying pan over medium high heat. 4. Add half of garlic to wok and sauté until fragrant. 5. Add the beef and stir-fry until no longer pink. Transfer beef to a plate. 6. Wipe pan clean and heat up 1 tablespoon oil. 7. Stir in garlic. 8. Add bell pepper(s) and stir-fry for 1 minute. 9. Stir in bamboo shoots and stir-fry for about 1 minute. Add 1 or 2 tablespoons water or broth, as needed, if mixture is too dry. 10. Stir in the sauce and bring to a boil. 11. Return cooked beef to wok. 12. Add green onions. 13. Stir-fry until everything is well-mixed and cooked through (about 1 minute). 14. Serve with rice.

Black Pepper Steak with Bell Pepper

Prep Time: 5 minutes | Cook Time: 10 minutes | Serves: 2

2 tablespoons vegetable oil, divided
1 pound flank steak, sliced thinly against the grain
1 thumb ginger, minced
2 cloves garlic, minced
1 small onion, chopped
2 red or green bell peppers, sliced

For the Marinade:
1 tablespoon soy sauce
1 tablespoon Chinese cooking wine
1 tablespoon cornstarch

For the Sauce:
½ cup beef broth
2 tablespoons soy sauce
2 tablespoons Chinese cooking wine
1 teaspoon dark soy sauce
1 tablespoon cornstarch
2 teaspoons sugar
Salt and pepper, to taste

1. In a bowl, combine marinade ingredients. Add beef and toss to coat with mixture, then let marinate for 15 minutes. 2. Combine sauce ingredients in a bowl. Set aside. 3. Heat 1 tablespoon oil in a wok, skillet, or frying pan over medium high heat. 4. Lay beef slices on hot oil for about 1 minute or until browned underneath. 5. Flip over and let cook until surface is no longer pink (about 30 seconds). Transfer to a plate. 6. Heat the remaining oil in the same skillet. 6. Stir-fry ginger and garlic until fragrant (about 30 seconds). Add onion and bell peppers. Stir-fry for about 20 seconds. 7. Give the reserved sauce a quick stir and add to the wok. 8. Stir continuously until sauce thickens. 9. Add beef and stir to coat with sauce. 10. Immediately remove from heat and serve over rice or noodles.

Garlic Beef with Snow Peas

Prep Time: 5 minutes | Cook Time: 15 minutes | Serves: 8

1½ pounds beef flank steak, sliced thinly
2–3 tablespoons vegetable oil, divided
½ pound fresh snow peas, ends trimmed
6–7 green onions, sliced
2 cloves garlic, minced
Red pepper flakes, for sprinkling

For Marinade/Sauce:
⅓ cup soy sauce
3 tablespoons cooking sherry
3 tablespoons brown sugar
2 tablespoons cornstarch
1-inch piece of fresh ginger, peeled and minced

1. In a bowl, toss the marinade ingredients with the beef. Set aside. When ready to cook, separate the beef while reserving marinade. 2. Heat the oil in a wok, skillet, or frying pan over medium-high heat. 3. Add the snow peas and stir-fry until color darkens (about 1 minute). Transfer to a plate. 4. Add more oil to wok as needed and heat to almost smoking. 5. Lay the beef on wok and let cook until underside is browned (about 1 minute) 6. Flip over and let cook until no longer pink. 7. Add the green onions and garlic to cook until fragrant. 8. Add the reserved marinade and give a few stirs. 9. Sprinkle with the red pepper flakes and serve with rice or noodles.

Chapter 5 Fish and Seafood

Nutritious Shrimp with Grains & Egg

Prep Time: 5 minutes | Cook Time: 11 minutes | Serves: 4

4 tablespoons vegetable oil, divided
2 star anise pods
½ teaspoon red pepper flakes
4 shallots, thinly sliced
Salt, to taste
¾ pound large shrimp, deveined, peeled, and cut into bite-size pieces
4 cloves garlic, minced
2 tablespoons ginger, peeled and grated
3 cups cooked grain of choice (such as sorghum, quinoa, or barley)
1 tablespoon soy sauce
1 tablespoon unseasoned rice vinegar
2 teaspoons toasted sesame oil
4 eggs, fried
1 red chili, sliced
Fresh cilantro, chopped, for garnish

1. Add 3 tablespoons oil to a wok over medium high heat. 2. Add anise pods, red pepper flakes and shallots. Stir-fry until shallots are golden brown. Remove from the oil and drain over paper towels. Discard anise pods. Season shallots with salt. Set aside. 3. Adjust heat to high. 4. Add shrimp, garlic, and ginger. 5. Stir-fry until shrimp are opaque (about 3 minutes). Transfer to a plate. 6. Heat up remaining oil. 7. Spread grains over wok and press down with a spatula. Let cook until grains crackle (about 1 minute). 8. Flip over and press down again for about 1 minute. 9. Repeat flipping over and pressing down until grains are lightly toasted (about 2 minutes more). 10. Return shrimp to wok and toss. 11. Add soy sauce, vinegar, and sesame oil. 12. Continue tossing until liquid is absorbed (about 1 minute). 13. Top with the fried egg and sprinkle with the fried shallots, red chili, and chopped cilantro.

Easy Fish in Oyster Sauce

Prep Time: 5 minutes | Cook Time: 15 minutes | Serves: 4

1¼ pounds firm fish fillets, cut into pieces
2 tablespoons vegetable oil
2 teaspoons ginger, minced
½ red bell pepper, cut into thin strips
½ yellow or green bell pepper, cut into thin strips
7 ounces snow peas

For the Sauce:

1 teaspoon cornstarch
3 tablespoons oyster sauce
1 tablespoon soy sauce
1 teaspoon sesame oil
3 tablespoons water

1. Combine sauce ingredients in a bowl. Set aside. 2. Heat oil in a wok, skillet, or frying pan over medium-high heat. Lay fish over wok and let cook until one side is browned before flipping over (about 5 minutes). Transfer to a plate. 3. Stir-fry ginger, bell peppers, and snow peas until crisp-tender (about 3 minutes). 4. Add sauce and let cook until thickened (about 2–3 minutes). 5. Gently stir in fish and let cook until heated through. 6. Serve over rice or noodles.

Tasty Glazed Salmon Fillets with Orzo

Prep Time: 10 minutes | Cook Time: 6 minutes | Serves: 4

4 salmon fillets, 2 lbs
1 oz. canola oil
1 oz. soy sauce
8 oz. teriyaki sauce
8 oz. orzo pasta, precooked
2 garlic cloves, minced
2 tbsp olive oil, combined with garlic
½ C. red bell pepper, diced
⅓ C. parmesan cheese
8 oz. spinach, julienned

1. Before you do anything, preheat the grill and grease it. Coat the salmon fillets with soy sauce and brush them with the oil. Cook them in the grill for 4 min on each side. 2. Brush the salmon fillets with 2 oz. of teriyaki glaze. 3. Cook them for 3 min on each side. 4. Cook the orzo according to the directions on the package. 5. Place a large wok over medium heat. Heat the oil in it. Add the garlic with peppers and orzo. Cook them for 2 min. 6. Stir in the cheese until it melts. Turn off the heat and add the spinach. Stir them several times until the spinach wilts. 7. Serve your orzo with the glazed salmon fillets and the remaining teriyaki sauce. Enjoy.

Shrimp Fried Rice with Carrots

Prep Time: 10 minutes | Cook Time: 30 minutes | Serves: 4

2 tablespoons olive oil
1 pound medium shrimp, peeled and deveined
Salt and pepper, to taste
2 cloves garlic, minced
1 onion, diced
2 carrots, peeled and grated
½ cup canned or frozen corn
½ cup canned or frozen peas
3 cups cooked rice
1 large egg, scrambled and chopped (optional)
2 green onions, sliced

For Seasoning:

3 tablespoons soy sauce
1 tablespoon sesame oil
½ teaspoon ginger powder
½ teaspoon white pepper

1. Stir together the seasoning mixture in a small bowl or cup. Set aside. 2. Heat oil in a wok, skillet, or frying pan over medium high heat. 3. Stir-fry shrimp until opaque (about 3 minutes). Season with the pepper and salt and then transfer to a plate. 4. Add the garlic and onion to the wok and cook until onion is translucent (about 3 minutes). 5. Add carrots, corn, and peas. 6. Stir-fry until tender (about 3 minutes). 7. Add cooked rice, green onions, and seasoning mixture. 8. Continue cooking, mixing with a shoveling motion, until well-mixed and heated through. 9. Stir in shrimp and egg (optional) until heated through. 10. Serve hot.

Chinese Clams in Black Bean Sauce

Prep Time: 15 minutes | Cook Time: 10 minutes | Serves: 3-4

2 pounds clams, scrubbed, soaked in salted water (1 teaspoon: 1 cup water) for 3 hours
2 tablespoons Chinese fermented black beans, rinsed and drained
¼ teaspoon chili paste, or to taste
2 tablespoons vegetable oil
1 inch fresh ginger, peeled and minced
2 teaspoons fresh garlic, minced
1 tablespoon Chinese cooking wine
1 scallion, chopped

For the Sauce:

½ cup chicken broth or stock
1 tablespoon oyster sauce
2 teaspoons light soy sauce
1 teaspoon dark soy sauce
1 teaspoon sugar
½ teaspoon sesame oil

1. Combine sauce ingredients in a bowl. Set aside. 2. Mash the rinsed fermented beans with the back of a wooden spoon. Stir in chili paste. Set aside. 3. Heat oil in a wok, skillet, or frying pan over high heat. 4. Stir-fry ginger and garlic until fragrant (10 seconds). 5. Stir in black bean paste and cook about 15 seconds. 6. Add clams and cooking wine, stir-frying for 2 minutes. 7. Add the sauce, place lid, reduce heat, and let simmer until clams are all opened (5 minutes). Remove any that remain closed. 8. Stir in chopped scallion. 9. Serve over rice or noodles.

Classic Louisiana x Japan Ramen

Prep Time: 10 minutes | Cook Time: 6 minutes | Serves: 1

1 (3 oz.) packages shrimp flavor ramen noodle soup
6 large shrimp, skin and veins removed
1 tbsp butter
¼ tsp garlic powder
1 tsp creole seasoning
¼ tsp black pepper
½ tsp hot sauce

1. Cut the noodles in half and prepare it according to the directions on the package without the seasoning packet. 2. Place a large wok over medium heat. Warm the butter to melt in it. Sauté for 6 minutes in it the shrimps with the garlic powder, creole seasoning, and black pepper. 3. Pour the noodles with ¼ C. of the cooking liquid in a serving bowl. Top it with the shrimps and hot sauce and then serve it warm. 4. Enjoy.

Garlic Shrimp in Lobster Sauce

Prep Time: 10 minutes | Cook Time: 15 minutes | Serves: 4

¾ pound raw large shrimp, shelled and deveined
Salt, to taste
Sugar, to taste
2 tablespoons vegetable oil
1-inch piece ginger, peeled and chopped
2 cloves garlic, thinly sliced
1 cup chicken broth
½ tablespoon Chinese cooking wine
¾ cup frozen peas and carrots
¼ teaspoon white pepper ½ tablespoon light soy sauce
1 egg white, lightly beaten

For the Thickener:
1 tablespoon cornstarch
2 tablespoons water

1. Season the shrimp with salt and sugar. Set aside. 2. Stir ingredients for thickener in a small bowl or cup. Set aside. 3. Heat oil in a wok, skillet, or frying pan over medium heat. 4. Stir-fry ginger and garlic until fragrant (1–2 minutes). 5. Add shrimp and stir-fry until surface begins to turn opaque. 6. Pour in broth and cooking wine. 7. Bring to a boil. 8. Stir in frozen vegetables, white pepper, and soy sauce. 9. Adjust flavor, as needed, with salt and sugar. 10. Give the thickener a quick stir and gently pour into wok, stirring continuously. 11. Bring to a boil. 12. Drop egg into mixture and swirl three times with chopsticks or a spoon until white form threads. 13. Immediately remove from heat. 14. Serve with rice.

Healthy Stir-Fried Squid and Celery

Prep Time: 15 minutes | Cook Time: 7 minutes | Serves: 4

½ pound celery, sliced thinly
1 pound squid, cleaned
2 tablespoons vegetable oil, divided
1 red chili, seeded and chopped
2 cloves garlic, minced
1 tablespoon soy sauce
1 tablespoon Chinese cooking wine
¼ teaspoon ground pepper
Salt, to taste

For the Thickener:
1 teaspoon cornstarch
2 tablespoons water

1. Cut open body of squid and score in crisscross manner. Cut into strips. Set aside. 2. Heat 1 tablespoon oil in wok, skillet, or frying pan over high heat. 3. Stir-fry celery until color brightens (about 2 minutes). Transfer celery to a plate. 4. Add remaining oil to wok, still over high heat. 5. Stir-fry chili and garlic until fragrant (about 30 seconds). Add squid. 6. Stir-fry for 1 minute and then return cooked celery to wok. 7. Stir in the soy sauce, cooking wine, pepper, and salt. 8. Continue stir-frying until squid begins to curl. 9. Give thickener a quick stir and then pour into wok, stirring continuously. 10. When sauce thickens, remove from heat. 11. Serve immediately.

Tasty Halibut Fillets in Tau Cheo Sauce

Prep Time: 10 minutes | Cook Time: 30 minutes | Serves: 6

2 ounces Halibut fillets
6 garlic cloves, peeled and minced
8 green onions, chopped
3 tablespoons tau Cheo (black bean paste)
3 tablespoons cooking oil
1½ teaspoon sugar
1½ teaspoon coarsely ground black pepper

For the Marinade:
4 ½ tablespoon minced fresh ginger
3 tablespoon rice wine
1½ teaspoon sesame oil

1. Rinse the Halibut fillets and slice them into bite-sized pieces. 2. Blot dry with paper towels and set aside. 3. Combine the ingredients for the marinade in a deep dish, and then add the Halibut fillets. 4. Turn to coat, then cover and refrigerate for 30 minutes. 5. Once the fish is marinated, place the wok over a high flame and add the oil. 6. Add the fish and garlic, then stir fry until cooked through. 7. Stir the tau Cheo into the wok and stir until combined. 8. Stir in the green onions, black pepper, and sugar, then sauté until combined. 9. Transfer to a serving dish and serve right away.

Fresh Tilapia Fillets with Teriyaki Sauce

Prep Time: 10 minutes | Cook Time: 6 minutes | Serves: 5

1 tbsp oil
5 tilapia fillets
½ C. brown sugar
¼ C. seasoned rice wine vinegar
½ C. soy sauce
1 tsp fresh ginger, grated
½ tsp garlic, minced

1. Place a large wok over medium heat. Add the oil and heat it. Lay in it the tilapia Fillets. 2. In a mixing bowl: Mix in it the remaining ingredients to make the sauce. Pour the sauce all over the tilapia. Cook them until the fish is done and sauce is thick. 3. Serve your tilapia fillets with teriyaki sauce warm. Enjoy.

Ginger Kung Pao Shrimp with Cashew Nuts

Prep Time: 10 minutes | Cook Time: 5 minutes | Serves: 2

1 pound medium shrimp, peeled and deveined
2 tablespoons vegetable oil
1 large green bell pepper, seeded and sliced
1 tablespoon garlic, minced
1 (1-inch) piece ginger, peeled and minced
3 Thai chilies, seeded and halved
2 tablespoons roasted cashew nuts, for sprinkling

For the Marinade:

1 tablespoon Chinese cooking wine
1 teaspoon cornstarch
½ teaspoon salt

For the Sauce:

1 tablespoon sugar
2 tablespoons water
1 tablespoon Chinese black vinegar
1 tablespoon soy sauce
¾ teaspoon cornstarch
½ teaspoon sesame oil

1. Marinate the shrimp in marinade ingredients for 10 minutes. 2. Whisk together ingredients for sauce. Set aside. 3. Heat a wok over high heat. Swirl in oil. 4. Add bell pepper, garlic, ginger and chilies. Stir-fry for 1 minute. 5. Add the shrimp and cook for 2 minutes or until shrimp has turned opaque and changed in color. 6. Stir in sauce, cooking until thickened (about 30 seconds). 7. Sprinkle with the cashew nuts. 8. Serve hot with rice.

Fish in Ginger-Chili Sauce with Carrots

Prep Time: 5 minutes | Cook Time: 15 minutes | Serves: 2

2 white fish fillets, boneless and skinless, cut into 2-inch pieces
Salt, to taste
White pepper, to taste
1 tablespoon vegetable oil
1 tablespoon freshly grated ginger
2 cloves garlic, minced
1 chili pepper, finely sliced
1 medium carrot, peeled and sliced
2 tablespoons water
1 cup baby bok choy, washed and chopped roughly
¼ cup garlic chives, cut into 2-inch pieces
1 teaspoon chicken powder
1 teaspoon sesame oil

For the Thickener:

1 teaspoon cornstarch
2 tablespoons water

1. Stir ingredients for thickener in a small bowl or cup. Set aside. 2. Season the fish with salt and white pepper. 3. Heat oil in a wok, skillet, or frying pan over medium-high heat. 4. Stir-fry ginger, garlic, and chili until fragrant. 5. Add fish to wok and let sear. 6. Flip over. Cook until both sides are opaque (about 5 minutes). Transfer to a plate. 7. Add carrots and water. 8. Season with salt and white pepper. 9. Cover and let steam until carrot is tender (about 3 minutes). 10. Add baby bok choy, garlic chives, and chicken powder. 11. Let cook until bok choy leaves turn bright green. 12. Return fish slices to wok. 13. Stir thickener. Scoop out a teaspoonful and add to wok. 13. Add another teaspoonful, if needed, until sauce thickens slightly. Be careful not to add too much thickener. 14. Add sesame oil and stir gently. 15. Serve.

Flavorful Nutritious Steamed Fish

Prep Time: 5 minutes | Cook Time: 15 minutes | Serves: 4

2 tablespoons ginger, julienned
1½ tablespoons light soy sauce
2 scallions, cut lengthwise
1 small bunch cilantro
⅛ teaspoon salt
2 tablespoons hot water
2 tablespoons vegetable oil
⅛ teaspoon sugar
10-ounce fillet of white fish

1. Combine the salt, light soy sauce, sugar, and hot water in a small bowl. 2. Prepare a steamer. 3. Rinse your fish fillet and place it on a heat-resistant platter that will fit in the steamer. Place it carefully in the steamer and set the heat to medium. 4. Steam for 10 minutes, covered, until done. 5. Remove from the steamer and carefully drain any liquid that has accumulated on the plate. 6. Top the steamed fish with about a third of the ginger, onions, and cilantro. 7. Heat 2 tablespoons of vegetable oil in a wok over medium-high heat to create the sauce. 8. Fry for 1 minute with the remaining ⅔ of the ginger. Cook for 30 seconds after adding the white sections of the scallions. 9. Toss in the remaining scallions and cilantro, as well as the soy sauce mixture. 10. Cook for about 30 seconds after bringing the mixture to a boil. 11. Immediately pour this mixture over the fish and serve!

Spicy Ginger-Garlic Shrimp Stir-fry

Prep Time: 10 minutes | Cook Time: 15 minutes | Serves: 4

1¼ pounds large shrimp, peeled and deveined
1 teaspoon salt
1 tablespoon dark sesame oil
1 (2-inch) piece fresh ginger, peeled and minced
5 cloves garlic, thinly sliced
1 large red bell pepper, coarsely chopped
3 tablespoons Chinese cooking wine
2 tablespoons rice vinegar
2 large oranges, peel and pith removed, cut into segments
3 cups cooked short-grain rice
¼ small red onion, sliced thinly, for garnish
Green onion, chopped, for garnish

1. Sprinkle salt evenly over shrimp. Let sit for 10 minutes. 2. Heat oil in a wok, skillet, or frying pan over medium-high heat. 3. Add ginger and garlic. 4. Stir-fry until edges begin to brown (about 4 minutes). 5. Add shrimp and stir-fry until slightly opaque (about 2 minutes). 6. Add bell pepper and cook for about 2 minutes until crisp-tender). Stir in the wine and vinegar. Bring to a simmer. 7. Cook until sauce begins to thicken (about 1 minute). 8. Stir in orange segments and let heat through. 9. Garnish with chopped green onions and red onion slices. 10. Serve with rice.

Easy Honey Poached Tuna

Prep Time: 10 minutes | Cook Time: 12 minutes | Serves: 4

2 tablespoons cornstarch
2 teaspoons Sea salt
1 teaspoon freshly ground black pepper
1-pound meaty fish fillet, such as Tuna or Mahi-mahi, cleaned and cut into even pieces
1 tablespoon soy sauce
1 tablespoon honey
1 tablespoon apple cider vinegar
1 teaspoon toasted sesame oil
2 teaspoons chili sauce
1 scallion, julienned, both green and white parts

1. Mix the cornstarch with Sea salt and pepper. 2. Dip the fish fillet into the cornstarch mixture, and coat the fish evenly on both sides. Gently place the fish in your wok. 3. Bring water to a boil in another pot or kettle. It needs to be enough water to cover the fish in the wok fully. 4. Once the water comes to a boil, pour it over the fish so that it's completely covered. 5. Tightly cover the wok with a lid or aluminum foil. Poach the fish for 12 to 14 minutes. 6. While the fish is poaching, create the sauce by mixing the soy sauce, honey, sesame oil, apple cider vinegar, and chili sauce in a small bowl. 7. When the fish is ready, drain it and transfer it to a serving dish; pour the sauce over the fish.

Mud Crab with Scallions and Ginger

Prep Time: 10 minutes | Cook Time: 20 minutes | Serves: 2-4

2 medium size mud crabs, cut into 4 and washed
2 tablespoons cornstarch
Vegetable oil, for deep frying
6 green onions, cut into 1-inch lengths
1-inch piece ginger, peeled and minced
3 cloves garlic, minced
2 tablespoons Chinese cooking wine
1 teaspoon sesame oil
Soy sauce, for dipping

For the Sauce:

2 tablespoons oyster sauce
2 tablespoons water
2 cups chicken broth
Pinch of salt

For the Thickener:

1 tablespoon cornstarch
1 tablespoon water

1. Stir together sauce ingredients in a bowl or measuring cup. Set aside. 2. Stir thickener ingredients in a small bowl or cup. Set aside. 3. Place crab pieces in a bowl and sprinkle with cornstarch. Turn pieces over to coat. Set aside. 4. Half-fill wok with oil. 5. Bring temperature of oil to 325°F. If without a thermometer, dip a wooden chopstick or wooden spoon handle into the oil. If bubbles form around it steadily (not too vigorously), it is ready for frying. 6. Fry the crab for 5 minutes. Remove with a spider strainer or slotted spoon and drain over paper towels. 7. Carefully pour the oil in the wok into a heat-proof storage container, leaving about 1 tablespoon. 8. Adjust flame to high.
Add green onions, ginger, and garlic. Stir-fry until fragrant and beginning to brown (about 1 minute). 9. Return crabs to wok. 10. Stir in cooking wine and sesame oil. 11. Stir-fry while gradually pouring in sauce. 12. Cover and let simmer for 5 minutes. 13. Give thickener a quick stir and pour into wok. 14. Stir and cook until the sauce begins to thicken. 15. Turn off heat. 16. Serve with soy sauce for dipping.

Homemade Shrimp and Black Bean Sauce

Prep Time: 20 minutes | Cook Time: 10 minutes | Serves: 2

1 tablespoon oyster sauce
½ teaspoon sesame oil
⅛ teaspoon white pepper
1½ cups low-sodium chicken stock
1 teaspoon dark soy sauce
¼ teaspoon sugar
1½ tablespoons black beans, fermented and rinsed
2 tablespoons vegetable oil
¼ teaspoon ginger, minced
12 ounces shrimp, peeled and deveined
2½ tablespoons cornstarch plus 2 tablespoons water
1 scallion, chopped
4 ounces ground pork
1 clove garlic, minced
¼ cup green bell pepper, finely diced
1 tablespoon Shaoxing wine
1 large egg, lightly beaten

1. In your wok, bring 2 to 3 cups of water to a boil. 2. Meanwhile, combine the oyster sauce, chicken stock, sesame oil, dark soy sauce, sugar, and white pepper in a liquid measuring cup. 3. Once the water has been brought to a boil, add the ground pork and simmer for 1 minute, breaking up any clumps. 4. Using a fine-mesh strainer, remove from the wok and set aside. 5. Wipe down your wok and set it over medium-high heat. Combine the black beans, oil, ginger, garlic, bell pepper, and ground pork in a large mixing bowl. Stir-fry the mixture for a total of 20 seconds. 6. Toss in the prawns and pour the Shaoxing wine around the wok's heated sides. Stir for a further 20 seconds. 7. Stir the sauce mixture to ensure it's thoroughly combined before adding it to the wok. 8. Bring to a simmer and then gradually whisk in the cornstarch slurry until the desired thickness is achieved. 9. Pour the barely beaten egg over the sauce's surface. 10. Simmer for 10 seconds to set the egg, then incorporate the egg into the sauce with a few strokes of your spatula. 11. To serve, fold in the chopped scallion.

Lemony Garlic Prawns

Prep Time: 10 minutes | Cook Time: 10 minutes | Serves: 2

½ pound king prawns
½ chili pepper
1 onion
2 cloves of garlic
2 tablespoons lemon juice
1 tablespoon sesame oil
2 tablespoons soy sauce
Salt and pepper, to taste

1. First, finely chop the onion, chili pepper, and garlic and roast in hot sesame oil. 2. Then put the prawns in the wok and sear them again for 3 minutes. 3. Then add the spices, lemon juice, and soy sauce. 4. Season with the salt and pepper.

Healthy Scrambled Broccoli with Shrimp

Prep Time: 20 minutes | Cook Time: 15 minutes | Serves: 4

10 ounces broccoli florets
¼ teaspoon granulated sugar
12 ounces shrimp, peeled and deveined
½ cup low-sodium chicken stock
1½ tablespoons soy sauce
1 tablespoon oyster sauce
⅛ teaspoon white pepper
1 tablespoon Shaoxing wine
½ teaspoon dark soy sauce
½ teaspoon sesame oil
2 tablespoons canola oil
2 garlic cloves, chopped
1½ tablespoons cornstarch plus 2 tablespoons water

1. Boil 4 cups of water in a medium-sized pot. 2. Mix the sesame oil, sugar, soy sauces, chicken stock, oyster sauce, and white pepper in a bowl. 3. Cook the broccoli for 30 seconds in the boiling water and then remove. 4. Return the water to a rolling boil, then blanch the shrimp for 15 seconds. Remove the shrimp. 5. Heat a wok over high heat. Pour 2 tablespoons of canola oil into the wok, then add the garlic and Shaoxing wine. 6. Pour in the chicken stock. Return the shrimp and broccoli to the wok and bring the sauce to a boil. 7. Drizzle in the cornstarch slurry, stirring constantly, until the sauce thickens and sticks to the shrimp and broccoli. 8. Serve.

Traditional Tempura Donburi with Lemon Wedges

Prep Time: 35 minutes | Cook Time: 25 minutes | Serves: 4

For Dipping and Serving:
2 tablespoons soy sauce
¾ cup dashi stock
2 tablespoons mirin
¼ cup daikon radish, finely grated
4 cups Japanese short-grain rice, cooked

For Frying:
2 medium white onions, sliced into ½-inch rounds
1 sweet potato, peeled and sliced into thin rounds
2 small heads of broccoli, cut into florets
12 large shrimp, peeled and deveined
2 cups oyster mushrooms, cut into small pieces
Vegetable oil, for frying

For the Batter:
1¼ cups cake flour
1¾ cups ice water
2 egg yolks

1. Combine the dashi stock, soy sauce, and mirin to make the dipping sauce. 2. Blend the cake flour, ice water, and egg yolks in a bowl. 3. Put the oil in a wok on medium-high heat. 4. Place a wire rack on top of a sheet pan that has been lined with paper towels. 5. Dip a piece of vegetable or shrimp into the batter and cook it in the oil. 6. Fry everything in batches for 1 to 1½ minutes, rotating each item 3-4 times during the cooking process, then placing it on the prepared wire rack. 7. To make the tempura donburi bowls, start by spooning a base of steamed rice into each bowl. 8. Garnish each bowl with the vegetables and a few shrimp.

Homemade Delicious Prawn Laksa

Prep Time: 10 minutes | Cook Time: 40 minutes | Serves: 6

- 2 pounds medium prawns, peeled and deveined
- 12 ounces dried rice vermicelli
- 1 large onion, peeled and chopped
- 6 fresh red chilies, chopped
- 6 Kaffir lime leaves
- 9 Macadamia nuts, chopped
- 4 lemongrass stems, white parts, sliced
- 4 garlic cloves, peeled
- 1½ liters chicken broth
- 4 ½ cups coconut milk
- 1 cup fresh coriander leaves
- ⅓ cup cooking oil
- 4 ½ tablespoons chopped fresh mint
- 4 tablespoons freshly squeezed lime juice
- 3 tablespoons fish sauce
- 3 tablespoons sugar
- 2 tablespoons coriander seeds, toasted
- 1½ tablespoon cumin seeds, toasted
- 4 ½ teaspoons shrimp paste
- 3 teaspoons chopped fresh ginger
- 1½ teaspoon ground turmeric
- 1 lime, sliced into wedges

1. In a food processor, mix the ground coriander, cumin, turmeric, ginger, garlic, onion, macadamias, lemongrass, shrimp paste, and chili. Blend with ¾ cup of broth until pasty. 2. Place the wok over low flame and heat the oil. Stir fry the paste until fragrant, then add the remaining broth. Bring to a boil and then reduce to simmer. 3. Stir in coconut milk, lime juice and leaves, sugar, and fish sauce. Bring to a simmer, add the prawns, and simmer until cooked through. 4. Cook the Vermicelli according to package instructions. 5. Drain and divide into individual servings. 6. Add the prawn soup followed by the, mint, coriander, and sprouts. 7. Serve.

Yummy Chinese Shrimp Patties

Prep Time: 30 minutes | Cook Time: 15 minutes | Serves: 5

- 1 small carrot, blanched and chopped
- 1-pound shrimp, peeled, deveined, and minced
- 5 water chestnuts, minced
- 1 teaspoon ginger, grated
- ½ teaspoon salt
- 2 teaspoons oyster sauce
- ¼ teaspoon sugar
- 1 egg white
- ¼ cup cilantro, finely chopped
- 2 teaspoons Shaoxing wine
- ⅛ teaspoon ground white pepper
- 1 teaspoon sesame oil
- 1 teaspoon cornstarch
- 3 tablespoons oil, for pan-frying

1. Toss the shrimp, carrot, cilantro, water chestnuts, Shaoxing wine, grated ginger, ground white pepper, salt, sesame oil, oyster sauce, cornstarch, sugar, and egg white together in a mixing bowl. 2. Whip everything together for about 5 minutes or until all ingredients are fully incorporated. 3. Heat the oil over medium-high heat in a wok. 4. Take a large spoonful of the shrimp mixture and roll it into a ball with another spoon. 5. Reduce the heat to medium and drop the shrimp balls into the wok, flattening them into a disc as quickly as possible. 6. Pan-fry each side for 3 minutes on each side, or until golden brown. 7. Serve.

Tasty Scrambled Shrimp with Eggplant

Prep Time: 10 minutes | Cook Time: 15 minutes | Serves: 4

- 24 shrimps, shelled
- 3 Asian eggplants, thinly sliced
- 2 onions, diced
- 1 head of Bok choy, thinly sliced
- 2 garlic cloves, minced
- 2 tablespoons tamari
- 2 tablespoons dried basil
- 2 tablespoons grapeseed oil

1. Heat oil in the wok on medium-high heat and brown the garlic. 2. Add onion and sauté until translucent. Add Bok choy and eggplant and fry for 3 minutes. 3. Push everything to the sides. Put in shrimp, tamari, and basil and cook for a few minutes. 4. Mix everything and cook until warm. 5. Serve.

Savory Marinated Salmon Stir-Fry

Prep Time: 10 minutes | Cook Time: 10 minutes | Serves: 4

½ cup oyster sauce
2 tablespoons rice wine
1 pound thick, center-cut Salmon fillet, cut into 1-inch pieces
2 tablespoons cooking oil
2 garlic cloves, crushed and chopped
1 tablespoon crushed and chopped ginger
1 red onion, cut into 1-inch pieces
1 red bell pepper, cut into 1-inch pieces
2 baby Bok choy leaves separated
4 scallions, cut into ½-inch pieces

1. In a large bowl, whisk together the oyster sauce and rice wine. 2. Add the Salmon and let marinate while you stir-fry. 3. In a wok over high heat, heat the cooking oil until it shimmers. 4. Add the garlic, ginger, and onion and stir-fry for 1 minute. 5. Add the Salmon, reserve the marinade, and gently stir-fry for 3 minutes. 6. Add the bell pepper and stir-fry for 1 minute. 7. Add the Bok choy and stir-fry for 1 minute. 8. Add the reserved marinade and scallions to the wok and gently stir-fry for 1 minute. 9. Serve.

Nutritious Marinated Salmon

Prep Time: 10 minutes | Cook Time: 5 minutes | Serves: 4

½ cup soy sauce
¼ cup Shaoxing rice wine
1 tablespoon minced fresh ginger
1 teaspoon honey
1-pound fresh Salmon fillet, cleaned and patted dry
4 tablespoons brown sugar
⅓ cup uncooked long-grain rice
¼ cup black tea leaves, such as oolong
2-star anise pods
1 teaspoon cornstarch, mixed with 4 teaspoons cold water

1. In a large bowl, make a marinade by mixing the soy sauce, rice wine, ginger, and honey. 2. Cut the Salmon fillet into 2-inch pieces, and add the pieces to the bowl; toss to coat with the marinade. 3. Let the Salmon marinate for 15 minutes. 4. Line your wok with a large piece of aluminum foil, letting the excess foil hang over the edges of the wok. 5. Prepare the smoking layer by mixing the brown sugar, rice, black tea leaves, and star anise pods in a small bowl. Spread this on the foil at the bottom of your wok. 6. Set a wire rack or a metal steamer basket with little legs on top of the smoking layer. 7. Heat the wok over high heat until the smoking layer begins to smoke, about 5 to 6 minutes. 8. Gently place the marinated Salmon on the rack in a single layer, skin-side down. 9. Reserve the marinade to make the sauce for the fish. Reduce the heat to medium-low, cover the wok, and smoke the Salmon for about 10 minutes. Turn off the heat and remove the wok from the heat. 10. Do not remove the lid from the wok. Pour the marinade into a small saucepan and bring it to a boil. 11. Remove it from the heat, and slowly add the cornstarch mixture to the marinade, constantly stirring until the sauce thickens. 12. Remove the smoked Salmon from the wok and place it on a serving dish. 13. Drizzle it with the sauce and serve. 14. Serve.

Spicy Scrambled Sea Bass with Scallions

Prep Time: 10 minutes | Cook Time: 4 minutes | Serves: 6

6 (5 ounces) Sea bass fillets, with skin on
Sea salt and pepper to taste
3 tablespoons vegetable oil, divided
½ inch fresh peeled ginger, thinly sliced
2 garlic cloves, thinly sliced
2 red chili peppers, deseeded and slivered
1 bunch scallions, thinly sliced
1 tablespoon soy sauce

1. Season the sea bass with the salt and pepper and make a couple of small diagonal cuts in the skin of each fillet. 2. Heat a wok over high heat until a drop of water sizzles on contact and add one tablespoon oil. 3. In two different batches, fry the fillets, skin-side down, for 3 minutes or until the skin is crisp. 4. Turn the fillets over and cook for a further 30 seconds to 1 minute. 5. Transfer the fillets to a serving plate and cover with foil to keep warm. 6. Heat the remaining tablespoon oil and fry the ginger, garlic, and chili peppers for 1 minute or until fragrant. 7. Remove the wok from the heat, add the scallions, and toss to combine. 8. Add the soy sauce to the wok and stir. 9. Spoon the sauce from the wok over the Sea bass fillets and serve.

Chinese Five-Spice Shelter Shrimp

Prep Time: 30 minutes | Cook Time: 15 minutes | Serves: 4

¼ teaspoon white pepper powder
1-pound large shrimp
2 teaspoons Shaoxing wine, divided
7 cloves garlic, minced
3 red chilies, chopped
1 cup peanut oil
¼ teaspoon sugar
4 slices ginger, minced
2 scallions, chopped
1 cup panko breadcrumbs
½ teaspoon salt
⅛ teaspoon five-spice powder

1. Toss the shrimp with ¼ teaspoon of white pepper powder and 1 teaspoon of Shaoxing wine in a mixing bowl. 2. Heat 1 cup of oil in a wok and fry the shrimp in two batches for about 15 seconds each. Remove the shrimp and set them aside. 3. Reheat the oil and re-fry each batch for a second time, about 5-10 seconds each time. 4. Transfer the shrimp to a separate platter and set them aside. 5. Eliminate the wok from the heat and carefully scoop out about ⅓ cup of the oil into a heatproof container. 6. Simmer for 30 seconds on medium-low heat after adding the ginger to the oil. 7. Stir in the panko and cook for another 30 seconds before adding the garlic and chilies. 8. Combine the shrimp, sugar, salt, 1 teaspoon Shaoxing wine, scallions, ¼ teaspoon white pepper, and ⅛ teaspoon five-spice powder in a large mixing bowl. 9. Toss everything together lightly and serve immediately.

Spicy Wok-Fried Squid

Prep Time: 10 minutes | Cook Time: 4 minutes | Serves: 4

2 tablespoons brown sugar
1 tablespoon soy sauce
1 teaspoon rice vinegar
2 teaspoons fish sauce
2 tablespoons water
1 pound squid, cleaned and cut into rings or 2-inch tentacles
1½ tablespoons peanut or vegetable oil, divided
2 Chinese dried red chilis
2 garlic cloves, minced
1 teaspoon minced ginger
½ sweet onion, thinly sliced
1 green bell pepper, cut into strips

1. Mix the brown sugar, soy sauce, rice vinegar, fish sauce, and water in a small bowl. Set aside. 2. Bring a large pot of water to a boil. 3. Parboil the squid for 10 seconds. Drain it and set it aside. 4. Heat a wok on medium-high until it is hot. Add one tablespoon peanut oil to the wok, and then add the chilies, garlic, and ginger. 5. Stir-fry for about 30 seconds until it is fragrant, and then add the and sauce. 6. Stir everything for about 30 seconds to prevent it from burning. Add the squid to the wok and stir-fry for 30 to 40 seconds. 7. Quickly remove the wok from the heat. (Don't overcook the squid, which becomes rubbery when overcooked). 8. Transfer the squid and sauce to a plate, reserving one tablespoon of the sauce for the vegetables. Heat the wok over medium-high heat. 9. Add the remaining 1½ teaspoons of peanut oil to the wok, and swirl to coat the bottom of the wok. Add the onion, green bell pepper, and reserved sauce to the wok, and stir-fry until the vegetables are crisp-tender, 2 to 3 minutes. 10. Place the vegetables on a plate, and top with the squid. 11. Serve immediately.

Wok-Fried Spicy Octopus with Vegetables

Prep Time: 10 minutes | Cook Time: 25 minutes | Serves: 4

Sesame seeds to garnish
1½ tablespoons of garlic
1 teaspoon of ginger
1 tablespoon cane sugar
1 teaspoon of black pepper
1½ tablespoon of sesame oil
2 tablespoons of soy sauce
4 tablespoon of Korean red chili paste
1½ tablespoon of red chili powder
3 stalks of green onion
½ onion
½ cabbage, chopped
28 ounces of baby octopus

1. Boil the octopus for two minutes in hot water. 2. Combine the red chili paste, chili powder, soy sauce, cane sugar, black pepper, chopped garlic, and shredded ginger in a bowl. 3. Drizzle sesame oil into a wok. 4. Sauté the sesame oil and onion for 2-3 minutes together. 5. Pour in the soy sauce mixture after adding the cabbage. 6. Toss everything together until it's well mixed. 7. Mix in the blanched octopus. 8. Serve.

Fried Garlic Fish Fillets

Prep Time: 10 minutes | Cook Time: 14 minutes | Serves: 8

For the Fish:

1 egg white
2 tablespoons soy sauce
1 tablespoon Chinese shaoxing wine
2 pounds white fish fillets, cut into bite-sized pieces
1 cup all-purpose flour
3 cups vegetable oil
3 scallions, chopped
1 teaspoon sesame seeds

For the Sauce:

4 tablespoons sugar
¼ cup chicken broth
1 tablespoon soy sauce
1 tablespoon vegetable oil
1 small garlic clove, grated finely
2 tablespoons fresh lemon juice
½ teaspoon lemon zest, grated finely
2 teaspoons cornstarch
2 tablespoons water

1. For the fish: in a bowl, add the egg white, all-purpose flour, soy sauce and wine and mix well. Add the fish pieces and coat with the mixture evenly. Set aside for about 10-15 minutes. 2. For the sauce: in a bowl, add the sugar, broth and soy sauce and beat until well combined. 3. In another small bowl, dissolve the cornstarch in water. 4. Heat the oil over medium heat in a small wok and sauté the garlic for about 10 seconds. Stir in the broth mixture and cook for about 2-3 minutes, stirring continuously. 5. Stir in the lemon juice and zest and cook for about 30 seconds. 6. Add the cornstarch mixture and cook for about 30 seconds, stirring continuously. Remove from the heat and set aside to cool. Coat the marinated fish pieces with flour evenly. 7. In a deep wok, heat the vegetable oil over high heat and fry the fish pieces in 2 batches for about 3-4 minutes or until cooked through. With a slotted spoon, transfer the fish pieces onto a paper towel-lined plate to drain. 8. Now transfer the fish pieces onto a serving platter and top with sauce. 9. Garnish with the scallion and sesame seeds and serve immediately.

Refreshing Sweet and Sour Cod

Prep Time: 10 minutes | Cook Time: 10 minutes | Serves: 4

For the Fish:

¾ cup all-purpose flour
1 tablespoon cornstarch
¼ teaspoon baking powder
⅛ teaspoon ground turmeric
Salt and freshly ground white pepper, to taste
⅔ cup cold club soda
¼ teaspoon sesame oil
12 ounces Cod fillet, cut into 1-inch cubes
2 cups canola oil

For the Sauce:

¾ cup canned pineapple chunks
¾ cup canned pineapple juice
2½ tablespoons red wine vinegar
⅓ cup plus 2 tablespoons water, divided
2 tablespoons sugar
¼ teaspoon salt
1½ tablespoons cornstarch
¼ cup green bell peppers, seeded and cut into 1-inch cubes
¼ cup red bell peppers, seeded and cut into 1-inch cubes
¼ cup red onion, cut into 1-inch cubes
1 tablespoon ketchup

1. Add flour, cornstarch, baking powder, cornstarch, turmeric, salt and white pepper, and mix well in a bowl. 2. Add the club soda and sesame oil and mix until smooth. Coat the fish cubes with the mixture evenly. 3. In a deep wok, heat canola oil over medium heat and fry the fish cubes in 2 batches for about 3-4 minutes or until golden brown. 4. With a slotted spoon, transfer the fish cubes onto a paper towel-lined plate to drain. 5. Meanwhile, for the sauce: in a bowl, combine the pineapple, pineapple juice, vinegar, ⅓ cup of water, sugar and salt and mix well. Set aside. 6. In a small bowl, dissolve the cornstarch into the remaining water. Set aside. 7. In a large non-stick wok, add two teaspoons of the frying oil over high heat and stir fry the bell peppers and onion for about 1-1½ minutes. 8. Stir in the ketchup and stir fry for about 20-30 seconds. Stir in the pineapple mixture and cook for about 2 minutes. 9. Slowly add the cornstarch mixture, stirring continuously. Cook for about 1-2 minutes, stirring continuously. 10. Add the cooked fish cubes and gently stir to combine. 11. Serve immediately.

Lemony Trout Fillets with Onions

Prep Time: 10 minutes | Cook Time: 40 minutes | Serves: 2

1 pound Trout fillets
1 tablespoon turmeric powder
Salt, to taste
1 tablespoon lemon juice
3 onions
2 garlic cloves
2 tablespoons of ginger
2 teaspoons of cumin seeds
2 teaspoons of rice flour
Oil as per your need
1 tablespoon of red chili powder
1 tablespoon coriander powder

1. Carve the fish into bits and wash them with water. Marinate fish bits with some turmeric powder, salt, and one lemon juice. Set it aside. Take a blender jar. 2. Add the cumin seeds, garlic, ginger, and onion to it. Blend to make a paste. To create a dense paste, move the masala paste to a pan. 3. Add the red chili powder, coriander powder, rice flour, salt, and add two tablespoons of oil. Remove parts of fish now and cover the masala with even paste on the fish. 4. Let the fish marinate for 1 hour. Heat oil in a wok. 5. When the oil is hot enough, add the fish one by one and fry until they are cooked on one side and then turn to the next hand. 6. Switch the fish to paper towels until finished to extract excess fat. 7. Serve.

Spicy Szechwan Shrimp with Red Pepper

Prep Time: 10 minutes | Cook Time: 30 minutes | Serves: 4

4 tablespoons of water
2 tablespoons of ketchup
1 tablespoon of soy sauce
2 teaspoons of cornstarch
1 teaspoon of honey, raw
½ teaspoon of red pepper, crushed
¼ teaspoon of ginger, ground
1 tablespoon of vegetable oil
¼ cup of green onions, sliced
4 cloves of garlic, minced
12 ounces of shrimp, cooked and with tails remove

1. Using a large-sized bowl, combine your water, cornstarch, raw honey, red pepper, ketchup, soy sauce and ginger until evenly mixed. 2. Heat some oil in a large-sized wok over medium to high heat. Add in your minced garlic and chopped onions. 3. Toss constantly and allow to cook for no more than 30 seconds. 4. Toss in your shrimp and continue to cook until thoroughly coated with your oil. Then add in your sauce mixture and stir to combine it thoroughly. 5. Continue cooking until the sauce begins to bubble and is thick inconsistency. 6. Remove from heat and serve immediately. 7. Enjoy!

Stir-Fried Garlic Cod

Prep Time: 10 minutes | Cook Time: 16 minutes | Serves: 2

For the Cod:
8½ ounces Cod fillet
Pinch of salt and freshly ground black pepper, to taste
3 tablespoons cornstarch
2 tablespoons vegetable oil
2 scallions, sliced
1 (1-inch) piece fresh ginger, sliced thinly
4 garlic cloves, chopped
½ of red chili, sliced

For the Sauce:
¼ cup water
1 tablespoon light soy sauce
2 teaspoons sugar

1. Season the cod fillet with a pinch of salt and black pepper. Dust the cod fillet with cornstarch evenly. 2. Then shake the fillet to remove excess starch. Set aside. 3. For the sauce: in a bowl, combine all ingredients and mix until well combined. Set aside. 4. Heat the oil over high heat in a wok and sauté the scallions, ginger, garlic, and red chili for about 1-2 minutes. With a slotted spoon, transfer the scallion mixture onto a plate. Set aside. 5. In the same wok, add the cod fillet and cook for about 5 minutes per side. With a slotted spoon, transfer the cod fillet onto a serving plate. 6. Add the sauce over medium heat and cook for about 2-3 minutes in the same pan. 7. Stir in the cooked scallion mixture and cook for about 1 minute. 8. Pour the sauce onto the fish and serve immediately.

Chapter 6 Snacks and Appetizers

Spicy Cold Seaweed Salad

Prep Time: 10 minutes | Cook Time: 20 minutes | Serves: 8

12 ounces fresh kelp
4 cloves garlic
3 thin slices of ginger
3 Thai chilies, thinly sliced
2 scallions, chopped, white and green parts separated
3 tablespoons vegetable oil
1 tablespoon Sichuan peppercorns
1½ teaspoons sugar
2 teaspoons Chinese black vinegar, or to taste
2½ tablespoons light soy sauce
1 teaspoon oyster sauce
½–1 teaspoon sesame oil, to taste
¼ teaspoon salt, or to taste
¼ teaspoon five-spice powder
1 tablespoon cilantro

1. Bring the water in a saucepan to a boil. Add the kelp and cook for 5 minutes over medium heat. Drain and rinse in the cold water. 2. Arrange the Thai chilies, minced garlic, ginger, and white sections of the scallions in the bottom of a large heat-proof bowl. 3. Pour 3 tablespoons of oil into a wok. Allow the Sichuan peppercorns to soak in the oil for 10 minutes over low heat until fragrant. 4. Remove the peppercorns and increase the heat on the oil until it's barely smoking. Then remove the pan from the heat and pour the oil over the aromatics in the heat-resistant bowl. 5. Return the mixture to the wok. Add the sugar, vinegar, light soy sauce, oyster sauce, sesame oil, salt, and five-spice powder. Stir in the green parts of the scallions and the cilantro until thoroughly combined. 6. Toss the kelp with the dressing to coat it. Serve.

Yummy Buttered Egg Puffs

Prep Time: 10 minutes | Cook Time: 20 minutes | Serves: 8

½ cup water
2 teaspoons unsalted butter
¼ cup sugar, divided
Kosher salt to taste
½ cup all-purpose unbleached flour
3 cups vegetable oil
2 large eggs, beaten

1. In a small saucepan, heat the water, two teaspoons of sugar, butter, and a pinch of salt to taste over medium-high heat. Bring to a boil and add the flour to stir. 2. Continue stirring the flour with a wooden spoon until the mixture looks like mashed potatoes and a thin film of dough has developed on the bottom of the pan. 3. Turn off the heat and transfer the dough to a large mixing bowl. Cool the dough for about 5 minutes, stirring occasionally. 4. While the dough cools, pour the oil into the wok; the oil should be about 1 to 1½ inches deep. 5. Bring the oil to 375°F over medium-high heat. 6. Pour the beaten eggs into the dough in two batches, vigorously stirring the eggs into the dough before adding the next batch. 7. When all the eggs have been incorporated, the batter should look shiny. 8. Using two tablespoons, scoop the batter with one and use the other to gently nudge the batter off the spoon into the hot oil. 9. Let the puffs fry for 8 to 10 minutes, often flipping, until the puffs swell to 3 times their original size and turn golden brown and crispy. 10. Transfer the puffs to a paper towel-lined plate using a wok skimmer and cool for 2 to 3 minutes. 11. Place the remaining sugar in a bowl and toss the puffs in it. 12. Serve warm.

Savory Wok-Fried Salty Peanuts

Prep Time: 35 minutes | Cook Time: 10 minutes | Serves: 6

Ingredients:
6 ounces shelled raw red-skin peanuts
Neutral-flavored oil
Sea salt

1. Rinse the peanuts under running water in a sieve. Allow at least 30 minutes for them to air dry in a single layer. 2. Add the air-dried peanuts to a clean wok with just enough oil to cover the peanuts. Then reduce the heat to a medium-low setting. Push the peanuts around gently and carefully to ensure equal heating and avoid burning. 3. As the moisture in the peanuts cooks out, little bubbles will emerge in the oil, followed by steam. When the popping sound stops and the pink skins on the peanuts become a mahogany brown, they're done. 4. Remove the pan from the heat, sieve the peanuts, and spread them to cool completely on a baking sheet. Serve with a pinch of salt.

Golden Brown Banana Fritters

Prep Time: 10 minutes | Cook Time: 15 minutes | Serves: 4

½ cup rice flour
¼ cup cornstarch
1 teaspoon baking powder
1 teaspoon sugar
½ teaspoon salt
½–1 cup ice cold water
Cooking oil for frying
6–8 bananas, peeled

1. Combine the rice flour, baking powder, sugar, cornstarch, and salt in a large mixing bowl. 2. Slowly sprinkle ice-cold water into the dry ingredients while mixing until you get a pancake batter consistency. 3. In a wok, heat the cooking oil to 325°F. 4. Coat the bananas in the batter before deep-frying them in small batches till golden brown. 5. Using a spider skimmer, remove the bananas from the wok. Place on paper towels or a cooling rack to remove any excess oil. 6. Serve while the bananas are still warm. Enjoy!

Coconut Rice Pudding with Nuts

Prep Time: 10 minutes | Cook Time: 30 minutes | Serves: 2

½ cup of rice
3 cups of full-fat milk
1 cup of coconut milk
½ cup of sugar
½ teaspoon of green cardamom
1 tablespoon oil
1 spoonful of cashews (chopped)
1 spoonful of pistachios (chopped)
1 tablespoon of almonds (chopped)
1 teaspoon of saffron

1. Soak the rice that you are using for 30 minutes. 2. Add the milk, coconut milk, saffron, and the rice into a wok and boil it. 3. Reduce the heat and insert the sugar and cardamom. Cook until the rice is smooth. Stir regularly. 4. If it is becoming too hot, add some more sugar. Let it cool off. 5. Serve.

Sesame Rice Ball

Prep Time: 2 hours 10 minutes | Cook Time: 10 minutes | Serves: 4

For Filling:
10 ounces Mung beans (peeled)
½ cup sugar
½ cup water (warm)
½ cup coconut (shredded)

For Dough:
2 cups water or more
1 cup sugar
1 cup rice flour
2 teaspoons of baking powder
½ cup of mashed potato flakes
2 tablespoons sesame seeds

1. Soak mung beans in warm water for at least 1 hour, then steam for about 20 minutes. 2. Meanwhile, dissolve the sugar in a bowl of warm water. Shift the cooled mung bean to a mixing bowl and coarsely mash it. 3. Mix in the sugar water mixture and the coconut thoroughly. The consistency should be similar to mashed potatoes. 4. Allow cooling before forming tiny quarter-size mung beanballs. Stir together the sugar mixture and the mashed potato flakes in a big mixing bowl to dissolve. 5. Add baking powder until it is fully dissolved. Combine the two forms of rice flour and stir to create a dough disk. The dough should have the strength of wet playdough. 6. Take off a slice of dough the size of a golf ball and knead it into a ball. Through the palms of your hands, flatten the dough into a disk and thin out the sides to create a pancake. 7. Add a couple of teaspoons of ¼ cup of water to the dough at a time, combining thoroughly after each addition. 8. Arrange the filling in the middle and fold the dough edges together, sealing the seams with your palms. Toss in a bowl of sesame seeds until fully covered. 9. Enable to rest for at least 1 hour, wrapped loosely at room temperature. 10. Fry it in a wok filled with hot oil. It is fine to fry many at once unless you want them to be fully immersed in oil for even cooking. 11. Remove and serve.

Garlic Sweet Chili Edamame with Sesame Seeds

Prep Time: 10 minutes | Cook Time: 15 minutes | Serves: 4

4 cups water
3 tablespoons salt
½ pound frozen edamame pods
1 tablespoon cooking oil
2 cloves garlic, minced
2 tablespoons sweet chili sauce
1 teaspoon toasted sesame seeds

1. In a medium-sized pot over medium-high heat, add the salt to the water and bring it to a boil. 2. Add the frozen edamame pods and boil them for 4 minutes. 3. Drain and rinse the edamame with cool water. 4. Heat the cooking oil over medium-high heat in a wok. 5. Stir-fry the edamame for about 1 minute in the wok. 6. Stir in the garlic and cook until fragrant (about 30 seconds). 7. Pour the chili sauce on top of the edamame, then sprinkle the toasted sesame seeds on top. To incorporate all of the ingredients, stir them together thoroughly. 8. Before serving, let the edamame cool a little. Enjoy!

Quick Egg Noodles

Prep Time: 10 minutes | Cook Time: 15 minutes | Serves: 4

4 ounces fresh uncooked egg noodles
2 cups vegetable oil
Salt, to taste

1. Heat the oil in a wok. 2. Take a tiny handful of noodles and drop them into the oil with care. Break them up with a pair of wooden or bamboo chopsticks as soon as they contact the oil to avoid them from staying together as they fry and expand. 3. Cook for 20 to 30 seconds on each side. Carefully flip the noodles using chopsticks or a slotted spoon and cook for another 20 seconds, or until equally golden brown. 4. Drain the excess oil from the fried noodles and set them aside to cool on a dish or a sheet pan coated with paper towels. Season the noodles with salt to taste. 5. Repeat until all of your noodles have been fried.

Easy Spicy Bamboo Shoot Salad

Prep Time: 10 minutes | Cook Time: 5 minutes | Serves: 4

7 ounces thin poached spring bamboo shoots
1–2 cloves garlic, minced
2 teaspoons Sichuan chili flakes
2 tablespoons vegetable oil
½ teaspoon sugar
½ teaspoon oyster sauce
1 teaspoon rice vinegar
1 teaspoon light soy sauce
¼ teaspoon Sichuan peppercorn oil
Salt, to taste

1. Using your hands, tear the bamboo shoots into thin strips. 2. Combine the garlic and Sichuan chili flakes in a small bowl. Heat the oil in a wok and add the garlic and flakes. 3. Add the sugar, oyster sauce, rice vinegar, light soy sauce, and, if using, Sichuan peppercorn oil. Toss in the shredded bamboo and serve. Season with the pepper and salt to taste and serve.

Sweet Coconut Corn Pudding

Prep Time: 10 minutes | Cook Time: 1 Hour 10 minutes | Serves: 6

For the Soup:
4 ears of corn
6 cups water
5 tablespoons of sugar

For the Coconut Milk Sauce:
1½ can of coconut milk
3 tablespoons of sugar
Salt as needed
½ teaspoon of cornstarch dissolved in 2 teaspoons of water

1. Remove the husk and silk from your corn and vigorously wash the cobs. 2. Break the corn kernels from the cob with a knife. 3. Put the corn cobs, sugar and 6 cups of water in a big wok and cook for around an hour. 4. In a small wok over medium heat, pour in all the coconut milk sauce and cook for a minute. 5. Stir in the coconut milk sauce when ready. 6. Serve.

Wok-Fried Vanilla Pears

Prep Time: 10 minutes | Cook Time: 10 minutes | Serves: 4

1 teaspoon of vanilla, pure
2 tablespoons of liqueur, orange
2 teaspoons of corn starch
¼ cup of water
¼ cup of white wine
Julienned rind and juice of ½ orange and ½ lemon
¼ cup of honey, pure
4 peeled, cored, sliced firm pears, ripe
4 tablespoons of butter, unsalted

1. Melt butter on high heat in a wok. Add pears. Stir fry for a minute. 2. Add the water, white wine, orange and lemon juice, and rinds and honey. Bring to boil. 3. Turn heat down to simmer. 4. Gently toss until pears become soft, which takes three minutes or so. Remove pears with a slotted spoon. 5. Dissolve corn starch in vanilla and liqueur. Stir into liquid in wok. Simmer 'til thickened lightly. 6. Pour this mixture over pears. 7. Serve them warm.

Easy Steamed Milk Custard

Prep Time: 10 minutes | Cook Time: 30 minutes | Serves: 4

1¼ cups whole milk
1 cup half-and-half
⅓ cup sugar
1 teaspoon vanilla extract
3 large egg whites
1 ripe mango, seeded and diced

1. In a medium wok, stir together the milk, half-and-half, and sugar over medium heat. 2. Warm the mixture, occasionally stirring, until the sugar has dissolved, about 5 minutes. Do not let the mixture boil or simmer. 3. Turn off the heat and stir in the vanilla. Set aside. 4. Beat the egg whites in a mixing bowl until frothy. Continue whisking while carefully pouring in the milk and stir to combine. 5. Pour the custard through a fine-mesh strainer into another bowl and then divide the custard among 4 (6 ounces) ramekins or custard cups. Cover the ramekins with aluminum foil. 6. Rinse a bamboo steamer basket and its lid under cold water and place it in the wok. 7. Pour in 2 inches of water, or until it comes above the bottom rim of the steamer by ¼ to ½ inch, but not so much that it touches the bottom of the basket. Place the ramekins in the steamer basket. 8. Cover the basket and steam over medium-high heat for 8 minutes. 9. Turn off the heat and let the custards sit in place for another 10 minutes before removing them from the steamer. The custards will appear set, with a slight wobble. 10. Place on a cooling rack and cool to room temperature before chilling in the refrigerator to set.

Homemade Coconut Banana Fritters

Prep Time: 10 minutes | Cook Time: 10 minutes | Serves: 2

1 egg, medium
1 cup coconut milk
To fry:
Canola oil
1 cup of flour, whole wheat
2 bananas, ripe

1. Mash the bananas in a large-sized bowl. Break the egg. Fold it in. 2. Add the flour to the mixture until it is thick enough that a spoonful will drop from a spoon easily. 3. Add some milk if the consistency is too thick. Adjust until it's right. 4. Heat the oil in your wok. Use a tablespoon to scoop the mixture from the steps above and drop it gently into the oil. 5. As soon as blobs change color, turn them over. Remove to drain and cover. 6. Work quickly through the banana mixture bowl, cooking four or five blobs at a time. 7. Serve when all are done.

Stir-Fried Sweet Crullers

Prep Time: 30 minutes | Cook Time: 10 minutes | Serves: 6

1¼ water
4 tablespoons of butter
1 tablespoon of sugar
½ teaspoon of salt
1 teaspoon baking powder
1 cup flour
4 eggs
For Glaze:
2 cups of sugar
¼ cup of milk

1. Combine the flour, baking powder, and salt. 2. Boil the water mixed with butter, sugar, and salt over medium-high heat. 3. Remove the pan from the heat and mix the flour mixture in it. 4. Return the pan to heat and cook for 3 minutes. Remove it from heat. Add 3 of the eggs to the mixture. 5. Mix it until the dough is soft and glossy and the eggs are well mixed in. Add another egg and blend until thoroughly mixed if the dough is already stuck to the beaters. 6. Using parchment paper, line a sheet pan. Place it in the shape you like. 7. Put it in the refrigerator. Make a glaze with the powdered sugar and milk. 8. Heat the oil in a wok for cooking. 9. Gently raise the dough circles from the sheet pan and put them into the hot oil. Fry until they turn brown. 10. Dip in the prepared glaze for 3 minutes or more. Let them cool, and they are ready to eat.

Lime-Marinated Calamari with Italian Parsley

Prep Time: 10 minutes | Cook Time: 4 minutes | Serves: 6

½ cup tequila lime marinade
1-pound calamari tubes, cut into 1″ pieces
2 tablespoons vegetable oil
1 tablespoon lime juice
2 tablespoons extra-virgin olive oil
2 tablespoons chopped Italian parsley
½ teaspoon Kosher salt

1. Combine the marinade with the calamari in a large bowl. Refrigerate for 5 minutes. 2. Heat a wok to medium-high heat and add the vegetable oil. 3. Swirl the oil around the wok and add the calamari. Toss and stir-fry the calamari for 4 minutes. 4. Remove the calamari to a plate and drizzle with lime juice, olive oil, and parsley. 5. Season with the salt to taste and serve immediately.

Easy Fried Sweet Bananas

Prep Time: 10 minutes | Cook Time: 10 minutes | Serves: 2

4 bananas, peeled and cut into halves, lengthwise
4 tablespoons plain flour
4 tablespoons rice flour
1 tablespoon cornflour
Pinch of baking powder
½ cup water
A pinch of salt
Oil for deep-frying
2 tablespoon brown sugar
Vanilla ice-cream

1. Mix the flour, rice flour, baking powder, cornflour, and salt with ½ cup of water into a smooth batter. 2. Heat oil in a wok 3. Dip the banana halves in the batter and deep fry in the hot oil until golden brown. 4. Drain the excess oil on paper towels. 5. Sprinkle with the brown sugar and serve.

Fried Cream Wontons with Scallions

Prep Time: 10 minutes | Cook Time: 20 minutes | Serves: 6

8 ounces cream cheese
2 teaspoons sugar
½ teaspoon salt
4 scallions, chopped
1 pack wonton wrappers
Vegetable oil for frying

1. Mix the cream cheese with sugar, salt, and scallions in a bowl. 2. Spread the egg roll wrappers on the working surface. 3. Divide the cream cheese filling at the center of each wrapper. 4. Wet the edges of the wrapper, fold the two sides, then roll the wrappers into an egg roll. 5. Add the oil to a deep wok to 325°F, then deep fry the egg rolls until golden brown. 6. Transfer the golden egg rolls to a plate lined with a paper towel. 7. Serve warm.

Sticky Coconut and Peanut Mochi

Prep Time: 10 minutes | Cook Time: 18 minutes | Serves: 16

For the Dough:
2 tablespoons vegetable oil
1½ cups sweet rice flour
¼ cup cornstarch
¼ cup caster sugar
1½ cups coconut milk
2 tablespoons coconut oil

For the Filling:
½ cup peanuts
½ cup coconut flakes, chopped
3 tablespoons sugar
1 tablespoon melted coconut oil

For the Coconut Peanut Mochi:
A large piece of wax paper
1 cup coconut flakes, chopped
16 small paper cupcake cups

1. Add the peanuts to a Mandarin wok and roast them for 3 to 5 minutes until golden brown. Allow the peanuts to cool, then chop them finely. 2. Layer an 11-inch by 11-inch cake pan with wax paper and brush with vegetable oil. sugar, cornstarch, Whisk rice flour, coconut oil, and coconut milk in a bowl. 3. Boil the water in a suitable wok, place the steam rack inside and add the dough to the steamer. Cover and cook for 15 minutes in the steamer, then allow the dough to cool. 4. Meanwhile, mix the peanuts with one tablespoon coconut oil, sugar, and coconut flakes in a bowl. 5. Spread the prepared dough in the prepared pan and cut it into 16 squares. 6. Add a tablespoon of the filling at the center of each square. Pinch the edges of each square and roll it into a ball. 7. Coat all the balls with coconut flakes and place them in the cupcake cup. Leave them for 20 minutes. Serve.

Caramel Cinnamon Caramel Granola

Prep Time: 10 minutes | Cook Time: 5 minutes | Serves: 8

2 cups of quick-boiling oats
1 cup of brown sugar
2 tablespoons of ground cinnamon
½ cup melted butter
5 tablespoons of caramel sauce
2 tablespoons of white sugar

1. Mix the oats, brown sugar, and cinnamon in a wok over high heat, cook for 5 to 10 minutes. 2. Remove from heat and add butter and caramel sauce; stir evenly. 3. Spread the mixture in a thin layer on a flat plate or baking sheet. 4. Sprinkle the white sugar over the muesli. Let cool completely before serving.

Homemade Eggy Scallion Dumplings

Prep Time: 10 minutes | Cook Time: 15 minutes | Serves: 4

2 tablespoons vegetable or peanut oil
½ teaspoon toasted sesame oil
1 teaspoon minced garlic
4 large eggs, beaten
Sea salt to taste
Freshly ground black pepper to taste
2 scallions, trimmed and chopped
24 to 30 dumpling, gyoza, or pot sticker wrappers

1. To a hot wok, add the vegetable oil and sesame oil. Add the garlic and cook for about 30 seconds. 2. Add the eggs to the wok, and season with the sea salt and pepper. 3. Scramble the eggs with a heat-proof spatula for about 30 seconds, or until done. Add the scallions and mix with the scrambled eggs. Transfer the eggs to a plate and set aside to cool until they can be handled. 4. Spoon a heaping teaspoon of the egg and scallion filling into the center of a dumpling wrapper. Wet the edges of the wrapper with the water, fold the wrapper to enclose the filling, and seal the dumpling by pinching the wrapper at its edges. Repeat with the remaining wrappers and filling. Make sure the uncooked dumplings don't touch each other. They will stick together until they're cooked. 5. Steam, pan-fry, boil, or deep-fry the dumplings, or use them in soup. 6. Serve.

Shrimp Dumplings with Bamboo Shoots

Prep Time: 10 minutes | Cook Time: 8 minutes | Serves: 4

½ pound (227g) raw shrimp, peeled, deveined
1 teaspoon oyster sauce
1 tablespoon vegetable oil
¼ teaspoon white pepper
1 teaspoon sesame oil
¼ teaspoon salt
1 teaspoon sugar
½ teaspoon ginger, minced
¼ cup bamboo shoots, chopped
12 dumpling wrappers

1. Blend shrimp with all the filling ingredients (except bamboo shoots) in a blender. Add bamboo shoots to the blended filling and mix well. Cover and refrigerate this filling for 1 hour. 2. Meanwhile, spread the dumpling wrappers on the working surface. Divide the shrimp filling at the center of each dumpling wrapper. Wet the edges of the dumplings and bring all the edges of each dumpling together. Pinch and seal the edges of the dumplings to seal the filling inside. 3. Boil water in a suitable pot with a steamer basket placed inside. 4. Add the dumplings to the steamer, cover and steam for 6 minutes. 5. Meanwhile, heat about 2 tablespoons oil in a Mandarin wok. 6. Sear the dumpling for 2 minutes until golden. 7. Serve warm.

Delicious Spiced Popcorn

Prep Time: 15 minutes | Cook Time: 10 minutes | Serves: 4

For the Spice Blend:

1 whole star anise, seeds removed and husks discarded
6 green cardamom pods, seeds removed and husks discarded
4 whole cloves
4 black peppercorns
1 teaspoon coriander seeds
1 teaspoon fennel seeds
1 teaspoon ground cinnamon
1 teaspoon ground ginger
½ teaspoon ground turmeric
⅛ teaspoon ground cayenne pepper

For the Popcorn:

2 tablespoons vegetable oil
½ cup popcorn kernels
Kosher salt to taste

1. To make the spice blend: In a small sauté pan or skillet, combine the star anise seeds, cardamom seeds, cloves, peppercorns, coriander seeds, and fennel seeds. Heat the skillet over medium heat and gently shake and swirl the spices around the pan. Toast the spices for 5 to 6 minutes, or until you can smell the spices and they start to pop. 2. Remove the pan from the heat and then transfer the spices to a mortar and pestle or spice grinder. Cool the spices for 2 minutes before grinding. Grind the spices to a fine powder and transfer to a small bowl. 3. Add the ground cinnamon, ginger, turmeric, and cayenne pepper and stir to combine. Set aside. **4. To make the popcorn:** Heat a wok over medium-high heat until it just begins to smoke. Pour in the vegetable oil and ghee and swirl to coat the wok. Add 2 popcorn kernels to the wok and cover. Once they pop, pour the rest of the kernels and cover. Shake constantly until the popping stops and remove from the heat. 5. Transfer the popcorn to a large paper bag. Add 2 generous pinches of kosher salt and 1½ tablespoons of the spice blend. Fold the bag closed and shake! Pour into a large bowl and enjoy immediately.

Stir Fry Sweet Cinnamon Potatoes with Maple Syrup

Prep Time: 10 minutes | Cook Time: 1 hour 10 minutes | Serves: 3

3 medium sweet potatoes, peeled
¼ cup maple syrup
¼ cup brown sugar
2 tablespoons butter, melted
¼ teaspoon of cinnamon powder

1. Place the sweet potatoes in a wok. Fill it with water. Let it boil for 30 minutes. 2. Drain and let it cool slightly before peeling. 3. Preheat the oven. Mix butter, syrup, brown sugar, and cinnamon to a boil in a wok. 4.Pour the sauce over the potatoes. 5. Bake for 30-40 minutes. 6. Serve.

Crispy Buttered Egg Puffs

Prep Time: 10 minutes | Cook Time: 20 minutes | Serves: 8

½ cup water
2 teaspoons unsalted butter
¼ cup sugar, divided
Kosher salt to taste
½ cup all-purpose unbleached flour
3 cups vegetable oil
2 large eggs, beaten

1. In a small saucepan, heat the water, butter, 2 teaspoons of sugar, and a pinch of salt to taste over medium-high heat. Bring to a boil and stir in the flour. Continue stirring the flour with a wooden spoon until the mixture looks like mashed potatoes and a thin film of dough has developed on the bottom of the pan. Turn off the heat and transfer the dough to a large mixing bowl. Cool the dough for about 5 minutes, stirring occasionally. 2. While the dough cools, pour the oil into the wok; the oil should be about 1 to 1½ inches deep. Bring the oil to 375ºF (190ºC) over medium-high heat. You can tell the oil is ready when you dip the end of a wooden spoon in and the oil bubbles and sizzles around the spoon. 3. Pour the beaten eggs into the dough in two batches, vigorously stirring the eggs into the dough before adding the next batch. When all the eggs have been incorporated, the batter should look satiny and shiny. 4. Using 2 tablespoons, scoop the batter with one and use the other to gently nudge the batter off the spoon into the hot oil. Let the puffs fry for 8 to 10 minutes, flipping often, until the puffs swell to 3 times their original size and turn golden brown and crispy. 5. Using a wok skimmer, transfer the puffs to a paper towel–lined plate and cool for 2 to 3 minutes. Place the remaining sugar in a bowl and toss the puffs in it. Serve warm.

Sweet Creamy Almond Sponge Cake

Prep Time: 10 minutes | Cook Time: 20 minutes | Serves: 8

Nonstick cooking spray
1 cup cake flour, sifted
1 teaspoon baking powder
¼ teaspoon kosher salt
5 large eggs, separated
¾ cup sugar, divided
1 teaspoon almond extract
½ teaspoon cream of tartar

1. Line an 8-inch cake pan with parchment paper. Lightly spray the parchment with the nonstick cooking spray and set aside. 2. Into a bowl, sift the cake flour, baking powder, and salt together. 3. In a stand mixer or hand mixer on medium, beat the egg yolks with ½ cup of sugar and the almond extract for about 3 minutes, until pale and thick. Add the flour mixture and toss until just combined. Set aside. 4. Clean the whisk and in another clean bowl, whip the egg whites with the cream of tartar until frothy. While the mixer is running, whisk the whites while gradually adding the remaining ¼ cup of sugar. Beat for 4 to 5 minutes, until the whites turn shiny and develop stiff peaks. 5. Fold the egg whites into the cake batter and gently combine until the egg whites are incorporated. Transfer the batter to the prepared cake pan. 6. Rinse a bamboo steamer basket and its lid under cold water and place it in the wok. Pour in 2 inches of water, or until it comes above the bottom rim of the steamer by ¼ to ½ inch, but not so much that it touches the bottom of the basket. Set the center pan in the steamer basket. 7. Bring the water to a boil over high heat. Place the cover on the steamer basket and turn the heat down to medium. Steam the cake for 25 minutes, or until a toothpick inserted into the center comes out clean. 8. Transfer the cake to a wire cooling rack and cool for 10 minutes. Turn the cake out onto the rack and remove the parchment paper. Invert the cake back onto a serving plate so that it is right side up. Slice into 8 wedges and serve warm.

Chinese Tea-Soaked Eggs

2 cups water
¾ cup dark soy sauce
6 peeled fresh ginger slices, each about the size of a quarter
2 whole star anise
2 cinnamon sticks
6 whole cloves
1 teaspoon fennel seeds
1 teaspoon Sichuan peppercorns or black peppercorns
1 teaspoon sugar
5 decaf black tea bags
8 large eggs, at room temperature

1. Bring the water to a boil in a saucepan. Add the dark soy, ginger, anise, cinnamon sticks, cloves, fennel seeds, peppercorns, and sugar. Cover the pot and reduce the heat to a simmer; cook for 20 minutes. Turn off the heat and add the tea bags. Steep the tea for 10 minutes. Strain the tea through a fine-mesh sieve into a large heatproof measuring cup and allow to cool while you cook the eggs. 2. Fill a large bowl with ice and water to create an ice bath for the eggs and set aside. In a wok, bring enough water to cover the eggs by about an inch to a boil. Gently lower the eggs into the water, reduce the heat to a simmer, and cook for 9 minutes. Remove the eggs with a slotted spoon and transfer to the ice bath until cool. 3. Remove the eggs from the ice bath. Tap the eggs with the back of a spoon to crack the shells so the marinade can seep in between the cracks, but gently enough to leave the shells on. The shells should end up looking like a mosaic. Place the eggs in a large jar (at least 32 ounces) and cover them with the marinade. Store them in the refrigerator for at least 24 hours or up to a week. Remove the eggs from the marinade when ready to serve.

Homemade Ginger with Sugared Dessert Soup

Prep Time: 10 minutes | Cook Time: 10 minutes | Serves: 4

3 cups water
¾ cup granulated sugar
¼ cup light brown sugar
2-inch fresh ginger piece, peeled and smashed
1 tablespoon dried chrysanthemum buds
2 large yellow peaches, peeled, pitted, and sliced into 8 wedges each

1. In a wok over high heat, bring the water to a boil, then reduce the heat to medium-low and add the granulated sugar, brown sugar, ginger, and chrysanthemum buds. Stir gently to dissolve the sugars. Add the peaches. 2. Simmer gently for 10 to 15 minutes, or until the peaches are tender. 3. They may impart a beautiful rosy color to the soup. Discard the ginger and divide the soup and peaches into bowls and serve.

Fresh Milky Mango Pudding

Prep Time: 5 minutes | Cook Time: 0 minutes | Serves: 4

½ pound frozen mango chunks
¼ cup sugar
½ cup hot water
1 packet unflavored gelatin
½ cup evaporated milk
Raspberries or kiwi slices, for garnish (optional)

1. In a blender, purée the mango and sugar until smooth. 2. In a large bowl, mix the hot water and gelatin. Let it stand for a few minutes. 3. Add the evaporated milk to the gelatin, and stir until they are combined. Add the mango purée and mix until well combined. 4. Pour the pudding into individual small cups or ramekins. Cover each one with plastic wrap, and chill in the refrigerator for at least 2 hours. 5. Before serving, garnish each pudding with the raspberries or kiwi (if using).

Garlic Black Bean Sauce

Prep Time: 10 minutes | Cook Time: 10 minutes | Serves: 2 cups

½ cup fermented black beans
1 cup vegetable oil, divided
1 large shallot, finely minced
3 tablespoons peeled and minced fresh ginger
4 scallions, thinly sliced
6 garlic cloves, finely minced
½ cup Shaoxing rice wine

1. Put the black beans in a small bowl, cover with the hot water, and let them soak for 10 minutes to soften. Drain and coarsely chop the beans. 2. Heat a wok over medium-high heat. Pour in ¼ cup of oil and swirl to coat the pan. Add the shallot, ginger, scallions, and garlic and cook for 1 minute, or until the mixture has softened. 3. Add the black beans and rice wine. Lower the heat to medium and cook for 3 to 4 minutes, until the mixture is reduced by half. 4. Transfer the mixture to an airtight container and cool to room temperature. Pour the remaining ¾ cup of oil over the top and cover tightly. Keep in the refrigerator until ready to use. 5. This fresh bean sauce will keep in the refrigerator in an airtight container for up to a month. If you wish to keep it for longer, freeze it in smaller portions.

Chili XO Sauce

Prep Time: 15 minutes | Cook Time: 10 minutes | Serves: 2½ cups

2 cups large dried scallops
20 dried red chilies, stems removed
2 fresh red chilies, coarsely chopped
2 shallots, coarsely chopped
2 garlic cloves, coarsely chopped
½ cup small dried shrimp
3 slices bacon, minced
½ cup vegetable oil
1 tablespoon dark brown sugar
2 teaspoons Chinese five spice powder
2 tablespoons Shaoxing rice wine

1. In a large glass bowl, place the scallops and cover by an inch with boiling water. Soak for 10 minutes, or until the scallops are soft. Drain off all but 2 tablespoons of water and cover with plastic wrap. Microwave for 3 minutes. Set aside to cool slightly. Using your fingers, break the scallops up into smaller shreds, rubbing them together to loosen the scallops. Transfer to a food processor and pulse 10 to 15 times, or until the scallops are finely shredded. Transfer to a bowl and set aside. 2. In the food processor, combine the dried chilies, fresh chilies, shallots, and garlic. Pulse several times until the mixture forms a paste and looks finely minced. You may need to scrape down the sides as you go to keep everything uniform in size. Transfer the mixture to the scallop bowl and set aside. 3. Add the shrimp and bacon to the food processor and pulse a few times to finely mince. 4. Heat a wok over medium-high heat. Pour in the oil and swirl to coat the pan. Add the shrimp and bacon and cook for 1 to 2 minutes, until the bacon browns and becomes very crispy. Add the brown sugar and five spice powder and cook for 1 minute more, until the brown sugar caramelizes. 5. Add the scallop and chili-garlic mixture and cook for another 1 to 2 minutes, or until the garlic begins to caramelize. Carefully pour the rice wine down the sides of the wok and cook for 2 to 3 minutes more, until evaporated. Be careful—at this point the oil may spatter from the wine. 6. Transfer the sauce to a bowl and cool. Once cooled, separate the sauce into smaller jars and cover. The XO sauce can keep in the refrigerator for up to 1 month.

Sweet Cinnamon Caramel Granola

Prep Time: 10 minutes | Cook Time: 5 minutes | Serves: 8

2 cups of quick-boiling oats
1 cup of brown sugar
2 tablespoons of ground cinnamon
½ cup melted butter
5 tablespoons of caramel sauce
2 tablespoons of white sugar

1. Mix the oats, brown sugar and cinnamon in a wok or a large pan over high heat, cook for 5 to 10 minutes; remove from heat and add butter and caramel sauce; stir evenly. 2. Spread the mixture in a thin layer on a flat plate or baking sheet. Sprinkle the white sugar over the muesli. 3. Let cool completely before serving.

Tasty Scallion-Ginger Oil

Prep Time: 5 minutes | Cook Time: 5 minutes | Serves: 2 cups

1½ cups thinly sliced scallions
1 tablespoon peeled and finely minced fresh ginger
1 teaspoon kosher salt
1 cup vegetable oil

1. In a heatproof glass or stainless-steel bowl, toss the scallions, ginger, and salt. Set aside. 2. Pour the oil into a wok and heat over medium-high heat, until a piece of scallion green immediately sizzles when dropped in the oil. Once the oil is hot, remove the wok from the heat and carefully pour the hot oil over the scallions and ginger. The mixture should sizzle as you pour and bubble up. Pour the oil slowly so it does not bubble over. 3. Allow the mixture to cool completely, about 20 minutes. Stir, transfer to an airtight jar, and refrigerate for up to 2 weeks.

Homemade Steamed Scallion Buns

Prep Time: 20 minutes | Cook Time: 20 minutes | Serves: 8

¾ cup whole milk, at room temperature
1 tablespoon sugar
1 teaspoon active dry yeast
2 cups all-purpose flour
1 teaspoon baking powder
¾ teaspoon kosher salt, divided
2 tablespoons sesame oil, divided
2 teaspoons Chinese five spice powder, divided
6 scallions, thinly sliced

1. In a liquid measuring cup, mix together the milk, sugar, and yeast. Set aside for 5 minutes to activate the yeast. 2. In a large mixing bowl or using a stand mixer with a dough hook attachment on low, stir the flour, baking powder, and ¼ teaspoon of salt to combine. Pour in the milk mixture and mix for 30 seconds. Increase the speed to high and mix for 5 minutes, until a soft, elastic dough forms, or 6 to 8 minutes by hand. Turn the dough out onto a work surface and knead a few times by hand until smooth. Place in a bowl and cover with a towel to rest for 10 minutes. 3. Cut the dough in half. With a rolling pin, roll one piece out into a rectangle, 15 by 18 inches. Brush 1 tablespoon of sesame oil over the dough. Season with 1 teaspoon of five spice powder and ¼ teaspoon of salt. Sprinkle with half the scallions and press gently into the dough. 4. Roll the dough up starting from the long edge as you would a cinnamon roll. Cut the rolled log into 8 equal pieces. To shape the bun, take 2 pieces and stack them one on top of the other on their sides, so the cut sides are facing out. 5. Use a chopstick to press down in the center of the stack; this will push out the filling slightly. Remove the chopstick. Using your fingers, pull the two ends of the dough out slightly to stretch, and then coil the ends underneath the middle, pinching the ends together. 6. Place the bun on a 3-inch square of parchment paper and set inside a steamer basket to proof. Repeat the shaping process with the remaining dough, making sure there is at least 2 inches of space between the buns. You can use a second steamer basket if you need more room. You should have 8 twisted buns. Cover the baskets with plastic wrap and let rise for 1 hour, or until doubled in size. 7. Pour about 2 inches of water into the wok and place the steamer baskets in the wok. The water level should come above the bottom rim of the steamer by ¼ to ½ inch but not so high that it touches the bottom of the basket. Cover the baskets with the steamer basket lid and bring the water to a boil over medium-high heat. 8. Reduce the heat to medium and steam for 15 minutes, adding more water to the wok if needed. Turn off the heat and keep the baskets covered for 5 more minutes. Transfer the buns to a platter and serve.

Simple Egg Foo Young with Gravy

Prep Time: 10 minutes | Cook Time: 10 minutes | Serves: 4

For the Gravy:
¾ cup chicken broth
1½ tablespoons hoisin sauce
1 tablespoon cornstarch dissolved in 2 tablespoons cold water

For the Egg Foo Young:
3 to 3½ tablespoons peanut or vegetable oil, divided
3 or 4 shiitake or cremini mushrooms, thinly sliced
4 scallions, thinly sliced
1½ cups fresh bean sprouts
¼ cup chopped ham or Canadian bacon
1½ teaspoons soy sauce
1 teaspoon sesame oil
6 large eggs

1. Heat a wok over medium-high heat until a drop of water sizzles on contact. Add 1 tablespoon of peanut oil, and swirl to coat the bottom of the wok. 2. Add the shiitake mushrooms, scallions, and bean sprouts to the wok, and stir-fry them for about 3 minutes. Add the ham, soy sauce, and sesame oil to the wok, and stir-fry them for another 1 to 2 minutes. Remove the filling mixture from the wok and set it aside. 3. In a medium bowl, beat the eggs. Add the filling mixture to the eggs and mix to combine. 4. Heat the wok to medium-high, and add 1 tablespoon of peanut oil. Pour in one quarter of the egg mixture to make an omelet. Cook the egg mixture until it is golden brown, 1 to 2 minutes per side. Transfer the omelet to a plate. Repeat this step with the rest of the egg mixture to make a total of 4 omelets. For each subsequent omelet, use only 1½ teaspoons or less of the remaining peanut oil. 5. To serve, pour some gravy over each omelet.

Yummy Plum Sauce

Prep Time: 15 minutes | Cook Time: 60 minutes | Serves: 2 cups

4 cups coarsely chopped plums (about 1½ pounds)
½ small yellow onion, chopped
½-inch fresh ginger slice, peeled
1 garlic clove, peeled and smashed
½ cup water
⅓ cup light brown sugar
¼ cup apple cider vinegar
½ teaspoon Chinese five spice powder
Kosher salt

1. In a wok, bring the plums, onion, ginger, garlic, and water to a boil over medium-high heat. Cover, reduce the heat to medium, and cook, stirring occasionally, until the plums and onion are tender, about 20 minutes. 2. Transfer the mixture to a blender or food processor and blend until smooth. Return to the wok and stir in the sugar, vinegar, five spice powder, and a pinch of salt. 3. Turn the heat back to medium-high and bring to a boil, stirring frequently. Reduce the heat to low and simmer until the mixture reaches the consistency of applesauce, about 30 minutes. 4. Transfer to a clean jar and cool to room temperature. Refrigerate for up to a week or freeze for up to a month.

Chinese Sesame Steamed Egg Custard

Prep Time: 10 minutes | Cook Time: 10 minutes | Serves: 4

4 large eggs, at room temperature
1¾ cups low-sodium chicken broth or filtered water
2 teaspoons Shaoxing rice wine
½ teaspoon kosher salt
2 scallions, green part only, thinly sliced
4 teaspoons sesame oil

1. Whisk the eggs in a large bowl. Add the broth and rice wine and whisk to combine. Strain the egg mixture through a fine-mesh sieve set over a liquid measuring cup to remove air bubbles. Pour the egg mixture into 4 (6-ounce / 170-g) ramekins. With a paring knife, pop any bubbles on the surface of the egg mixture. Cover the ramekins with aluminum foil. 2. Rinse a bamboo steamer basket and its lid under cold water and place it in the wok. Pour in 2 inches of water, or until it comes above the bottom rim of the steamer by ¼ to ½ inch, but not so much that it touches the bottom of the basket. Place the ramekins in the steamer basket. Cover with the lid. 3. Bring the water to a boil, then reduce the heat to a low simmer. Steam over low heat for about 10 minutes or until the eggs are just set. 4. Carefully remove the ramekins from the steamer and garnish each custard with some scallions and a few drops of sesame oil. Serve immediately.

Chapter 7 Desserts

Quick Stir-Fried Bananas Foster

Prep Time: 10 minutes | Cook Time: 30 minutes | Serves: 2

Vanilla extract, one teaspoon
Cinnamon powder, a quarter teaspoon
Unsalted butter six tablespoon
Dark rum, a quarter cup
Dark brown sugar, one cup
Vanilla ice cream, as required
Peeled firm bananas, four

1. Take a large bowl. 2. Add the brown sugar, butter and cinnamon powder. 3. Beat your butter mixture until the brown sugar melts down. 4. Heat a wok. 5. Add your butter mixture into the wok. 6. Add the peeled firm bananas into the butter. 7. Cook your dark rum and vanilla extract into the wok. 8. When your bananas are cooked properly, dish them out. 9. Add the vanilla ice cream on top of your bananas. 10. Your dish is ready to be served.

Sweet Sesame Balls

Prep Time: 10 minutes | Cook Time: 10 minutes | Serves: 4

Glutinous rice flour, three cups
White sesame seeds, a quarter cup
Vegetable oil, two tablespoon
Brown sugar, two cups
Black sesame seeds, a quarter cup
Sweetened red bean paste, one cup

1. Heat a wok. 2. Add the vegetable oil in the wok. 3. Add the white and black sesame seeds. 4. Cook them for five minutes. 5. Add the glutinous rice flour and brown sugar into the wok. 6. Add the sweetened red bean paste into the mixture. 7. Cook your dish and then dish out. 8. When the mixture turns a little cold, make small round balls from the mixture. 9. Your dish is ready to be served.

Tasty Snow Skin Mooncakes

Prep Time: 30 minutes | Cook Time: 10 minutes | Serves: 4

Glutinous rice flour, three cups
Simple rice flour, one cup
Wheat starch, a quarter cup
Vegetable oil, two tablespoon
Brown sugar, two cups
Ground cinnamon, half teaspoon
Whole milk, a quarter cup
Sweetened red mung bean paste, one cup

1. In a bowl, add all the wet ingredients except the red mung bean paste. 2. Add the dry ingredients into a separate bowl. 3. Add the dry ingredients into the wet ingredients. 4. Take a cupcake mold. 5. Grease your mold and then add the mixture into the mold. 6. Add the mung bean paste into each cupcake. 7. Add the rice mixture on top again to cover the bean paste. 8. Steam your cakes in a wok. 9. Your dish is ready to be served.

Homemade Peach Squares

Prep Time: 10 minutes | Cook Time: 40 minutes | Serves: 2

Powdered sugar, one cup
Sugar, one cup
Vanilla extract, one teaspoon
Eggs, two
Peach slices, one cup
Salted butter, one cup
Walnut pieces, one cup
All-purpose flour, one and a half cup

1. Take a wok. 2. Add the salted butter into the wok. 3. Add the peach slices into the wok. 4. Switch off the stove. 5. In a bowl, add the sugar and eggs. 6. Beat the eggs and powdered sugar. 7. Add the vanilla extract and all-purpose flour and mix it. 8. Add the peach mixture and walnut pieces into the mixture. 9. Add the mixture into a dish. 10. Make sure the dish is properly greased. 11. Steam your dish in a wok for fifteen to twenty minutes. 12. Dish out your peach cake. 13. Cut them into square shapes and dust the powdered sugar on top. 14. Your dish is ready to be served.

Stir-Fried Spiced Apples Shortcake

Prep Time: 10 minutes | Cook Time: 40 minutes | Serves: 2

Ground cinnamon, half teaspoon
Chopped mixed peel, one tablespoon
Self-rising flour, one cup
Mixed spice, one teaspoon
Milk, one tablespoon
Baking powder, one teaspoon
Apple slices, three
Eggs, two
Butter, half cup
Brown sugar, one cup
Orange zest, half cup

1. Take a wok. 2. Add the butter. 3. When it melts down add the apple slices. 4. Cook your apples. 5. Switch off the stove. 6. Add the mixture into a bowl. 7. Add the rest of the ingredients and mix. 8. Add the mixture into a dish. 9. Grease your dish. 10. Add the dish into a wok full of water. 11. Make sure the water is below the level of the dish. 12. Cover the wok. 13. Steam your cake for fifteen to twenty minutes. 14. Your dish is ready to be served.

Tamari Mongolian Chicken

Prep Time: 5 minutes | Cook Time: 15 minutes | Serves: 4

Chicken, one pound
Cornstarch, one tablespoon
Cooking oil, half cup
Garlic powder, one tablespoon
Ginger, one tablespoon
Hoisin sauce, one tablespoon
Sesame oil, one tablespoon
Brown sugar, one cup
Tamari sauce, half cup
Red chili, to serve
Green onions, two
Salt, to taste
Black Pepper, to taste

1. Take a large wok and add oil in it. 2. Heat it over medium high heat. 3. Add the cut up chicken into it. 4. Add the ginger, garlic powder and pepper. 5. Cook it for one minute with the continuous stirring. 6. Add the green onions into the mixture. 7. Cook it for a few minutes. 8. Continue boiling for five minutes until water reduces to minimum level. 9. Add the sauce ingredients in a separate bowl. 10. Add the corn starch and brown sugar in the bowl. 11. Dissolve all the ingredients well. 12. Put all the ingredients together into the wok and cook well. 13. Your dish is ready to be served with the sauces that you prefer.

Easy Millet Congee

Prep Time: 20 minutes | Cook Time: 20 minutes | Serves: 2

Millet, one cup
Cream, two tablespoon
Butter, one cup
Eggs, two
Cherries, two
All-purpose flour, two cups
Water, as required
Baking soda, one tablespoon
Salt, a pinch
Pepper, to taste

1. Take a wok and clean it well. 2. Add the sugar and the baking soda and the millet into it. 3. Add the salt and cream. 4. Add the all-purpose flour into it so that congee can be smooth. 5. Add the crushed walnuts into the mixture. 6. Mix all the ingredients well. 7. Add beaten eggs into the mixture. 8. Pour into the dish and spread evenly. 9. Take a small bowl and add the butter. 10. Mix them until become smooth and then add it into your dish. 11. Add the salt as required. 12. Simmer it for about five minutes. 13. Your dish is ready to be served with cherries and the walnuts. 14. You can refrigerate your dish as well.

Simple Apple Cinnamon Coffee Cake

Prep Time: 30 minutes | Cook Time: 10 minutes | Serves: 4

Milk, two cups
Apple slices, two
Cinnamon, one tablespoon
Coffee, one cup
White sugar, half cup
Salt, one teaspoon
Eggs, two
Lemon extract, one teaspoon
Almond extract, one teaspoon
All-purpose flour, two cups
Butter, one cup

1. Take a medium bowl and add the sliced apples in it. 2. Add the coffee and cinnamon into it. 3. Add one cup flour and mix well. 4. Then refrigerate it. 5. Take a large bowl and add butter into it. 6. Add the sugar, salt and milk. 7. Mix them well. 8. Mix the warm milk mixture with the flour. 9. Add the eggs, lemon extract and almond extract together. 10. Stir it for few minutes. 11. Steam your cake in a wok for ten minutes. 12. Your dish is ready to be served.

Gingered Vegetable Dumplings with the Sauce

Prep Time: 15 minutes | Cook Time: 8 minutes | Serves: 15-20

For the Dumplings:
2 teaspoons olive oil
4 cups shredded cabbage
1 carrot, shredded
2 scallions, chopped
5 to 8 garlic chives, cut into 1-inch pieces
1-inch piece of ginger, peeled and minced
1 tablespoon water
2 teaspoons sesame oil, plus 2 teaspoons for brushing
Salt and pepper
15 to 20 round wonton wrappers

For The Dipping Sauce:
2 tablespoons soy sauce
2 teaspoons sesame oil
2 teaspoons rice vinegar
1 teaspoon chili oil
1-inch piece of ginger, peeled and finely minced

1. In a wok over medium heat, heat the olive oil. 2. Add the cabbage, carrot, scallions, garlic chives, and ginger to the wok. Stir-fry for about 1 minute. 3. Add the water to help steam the vegetables. Stir-fry until most of the water has evaporated. Drizzle 2 teaspoons of sesame oil over the vegetables. Season with the pepper and salt and toss. Remove from the heat and set it aside to cool. 4. Place about 1 teaspoon of vegetable mixture in the middle of a wonton wrapper. 5. Dampen the edges of the wonton wrapper with a little water, fold the wrapper in half so that it forms a triangle, and gently press down to seal the edges. 6. Brush the dumplings with a light coating of sesame oil. 7. Line a bamboo steamer with parchment paper liners or napa cabbage leaves. Arrange the dumplings on top and steam for 8 minutes, or until the wonton wrappers look slightly translucent. 8. While the dumplings are steaming, make the dipping sauce. Combine the soy sauce, sesame oil, rice vinegar, chili oil, and ginger in a small bowl. 9. Serve the dumplings with the dipping sauce.

Milky Mango Sago

Prep Time: 10 minutes | Cook Time: 10 minutes | Serves: 4

Milk, two cups
Mangoes, two
White sugar, half cup
Salt, one teaspoon
Eggs, two
Lemon extract, one teaspoon
Almond extract, one teaspoon
All-purpose flour, two cups
Butter, one cup

1. Take a medium bowl and add the mango slices in it. 2. Add the one cup flour and mix well. 3. Take a large bowl and add milk into it. 4. Add the sugar and salt as required. 5. Mix them well. 6. Mix the warm milk mixture with the flour and the yeast. 7. Add the eggs, lemon extract and almond extract together. 8. Stir it for few minutes. 9. Add the sugar to taste if required. 10. Your dish is ready to be served.

Yummy Sweet Rice Balls with Black Sesame

Prep Time: 50 minutes | Cook Time: 10 minutes | Serves: 4

Black sesame seeds, one cup
Butter, two cups
Warm water, half cup
Caster sugar, one cup
Rice flour, half cup
Oil, one tablespoon
Salt, to taste
Pepper, to taste
Ginger, two tablespoon
Pandan leaves, three

1. Take four cups of water in a wok. 2. Boil the water well. 3. Add the ginger, pandan leaves and sugar. 4. Boil the water until all ingredients are dissolved. 5. Toast black sesame seeds on a wok for ten to fifteen minutes. 6. Toast the seeds until they come in a powdered form. 7. Then you can add sugar and oil as required. 8. Take a large bowl and add flour in it. 9. Make dough with your hands. 10. Cook sweet rice in the end in a large wok. 11. Fill the rice balls with black sesame seeds. 12. Cook it for ten minutes. 13. Your dish is ready to be served.

Golden Almond Syrup

Prep Time: 10 minutes | Cook Time: 30 minutes | Serves: 2

Boiling water, two cups
Brown Sugar, half cup
Baking powder, half cup
Milk, half cup
Salt, a pinch
Almond extract, one tablespoon

1. Take a medium bowl and add the boiling water in it. 2. Add one cup flour and the rum extract. 3. Mix them well. 4. Take a large bowl and add the heavy cream into it. 5. Add the sugar, the salt and the milk. 6. Mix them well. 7. Add the eggs and the almond extract together. 8. Cook your mixture for few minutes in a wok. 9. Cook for ten minutes. 10. Your dish is ready to be served.

Snow Fungus Soup with Pears and Dates

Prep Time: 10 minutes | Cook Time: 15 minutes | Serves: 2

Dried goji berries, one cup
Dried snow fungus, one cup
Asian pear, one
Chinese red dates, one cup
Water, eight cups
Rock sugar, half cup
Vanilla extract, one teaspoon

1. Take a small wok. 2. Add the water and rock sugar. 3. When the sugar dissolves in the water, add the dried goji berries, dried snow fungus, Asian pear and Chinese red dates. 4. Add the vanilla extract into the mixture. 5. Cook your mixture for approximately ten to fifteen minutes. 6. Your dish is ready to be served.

Delicious Steamed White Sugar Sponge Cake

Prep Time: 10 minutes | Cook Time: 40 minutes | Serves: 2

Self-rising flour, one cup
Milk, one tablespoon
Baking powder, one teaspoon
Eggs, two
Butter, half cup
White sugar, one cup

1. Add all the ingredients and mix. 2. Grease your dish. 3.Add the mixture into a dish. 4. Put the dish into a wok full of water. 5. Make sure the water is below the level of the dish. 6. Cover the wok. 7. Steam your cake for fifteen to twenty minutes. 8. Your dish is ready to be served.

Healthy San Xian Wontons

Prep Time: 10 minutes | Cook Time: 20 minutes | Serves: 12

8 ounces shrimp; peeled, deveined, and chopped
8 ounces ground pork
8 ounces ground chicken
1 tablespoon ginger, minced
¼ cup scallion, chopped
2 tablespoons vegetable oil
2 tablespoons light soy sauce
1 tablespoon oyster sauce
½ tablespoon sesame oil
½ teaspoon ground white pepper
½ cup water
2 packages wonton wrappers

1. Sauté the scallions and ginger with the oil in a Mandarin wok until soft. 2. Stir in the pork, shrimp, chicken, and rest of the ingredients (except the wrappers). 3. Sauté for about 8 minutes, and then remove the filling from the heat. 4. Allow the filling to cool and spread the egg roll wrappers on the working surface. 5. Divide the pork-shrimp filling at the center of each wrapper. 6. Wet the edges of the wrapper, and fold the two sides then roll the wrappers into an egg roll. 7. Add the oil to a deep wok to 325°F and then deep fry the egg rolls until golden-brown. 8. Transfer the golden egg rolls to a plate lined with a paper towel. 9. Serve warm.

Authentic Chinese Chili Chicken Dry

Prep Time: 5 minutes | Cook Time: 30 minutes | Serves: 3

Chinese chili, half cup
Chicken, one pound
Cornstarch, one tablespoon
Cooking oil, half cup
Garlic powder, one tablespoon
Ginger, one tablespoon
Sesame oil, one tablespoon
Brown sugar, one cup
Red chili, to serve
Green onions, two
Salt, to taste
Black Pepper, to taste

1. Take a large wok and add oil in it. 2. Heat it over medium high heat. 3. Add the cut up chicken into it. 4. Add the ginger, garlic powder and pepper. 5. Cook it for one minute with the continuous stirring. 6. Add the green onions into the mixture. 7. Cook it for few more minutes. 8. Continue boiling for five minutes until water reduces to minimum level. 9. Add the sauce and the Chinese red chili in the wok. 10. Add the corn starch and brown sugar in the bowl. 11. Dissolve all the ingredients well. 12. Put all the ingredients together into the wok and cook well. 13. Cook until your chicken becomes almost dry. 14. Garnish your dish with cilantro and chili. 15. Your dish is ready to be served with the sauces that you prefer.

Traditional Sichuan Chicken and Vegetables

Prep Time: 30 minutes | Cook Time: 10 minutes | Serves: 4

Coconut cream, one cup
Chicken stock, two cups
Minced garlic, one teaspoon
Minced ginger, one teaspoon
Sichuan peppers, two tablespoon
Shallot, one
Kaffir lime leaves, four
Lime wedges
Lemon grass, two sticks
Fish sauce, two tablespoon
Mix vegetables, one cup
Coconut milk, one cup
Cilantro, a quarter cup
Chicken pieces, half pound
Olive oil, one tablespoon

1. Take a large wok. 2. Add the shallots and olive oil. 3. Cook your shallots and then add the chicken pieces. 4. When the chicken pieces are half cooked then add the chicken stock, minced garlic and ginger. 5. Add the Sichuan peppers and coconut milk. 6. Cook your ingredients until they start boiling. 7. Add in the mixed vegetables, lemon grass and rest of the ingredients into your dish. 8. Cook your ingredients for ten minutes. 9. Add the coconut cream in the end and mix it for five minutes. 10. Garnish it with cilantro leaves. 11. Your dish is ready to be served.

Butter Osmanthus Cake

Prep Time: 10 minutes | Cook Time: 25 minutes | Serves: 3

Osmanthus syrup, one cup
Cream, two tablespoon
Butter, one cup
Eggs, two
Blueberries, half cup
All-purpose flour, two cups
Water, as required
Baking soda, one tablespoon
Salt, a pinch
Walnuts, one cup

1. Take a large bowl and clean it well. 2. Add the sugar and the baking soda and the osmanthus syrup. 3. Add the salt and cream. 4. Add the all-purpose flour into it so that cake can be crispy. 5. Add the crushed walnuts into the mixture. 6. Mix all the ingredients well. 7. Add beaten eggs into the mixture. 8. Pour into the dish and spread evenly. 9. Take a small bowl and add the sugar and the butter. 10. Mix them until become smooth. 11. Add the salt as required. 12. Steam it for about twenty-five minutes. 13. Dish out your cake and then slice it. 14. Your dish is ready to be served. 15. You can refrigerate your cake as well.

Classic Chinese Sweet Peanut Cream Dessert

Prep Time: 50 minutes | Cook Time: 30 minutes | Serves: 4

Sweet peanuts, one cup
Sugar, two tablespoon
Cream, two tablespoon
Butter, one cup
Eggs, two
All-purpose flour, two cups
Water, as required
Baking soda, one tablespoon
Salt, a pinch

1. Take a large bowl and clean it well. 2. Add the sugar and the baking soda and the sweet peanuts into it. 3. Add the salt and the cream. 4. Add all-purpose flour into it so that dessert can be smooth. 5. Add the crushed peanuts and walnuts into the mixture. 6. Mix all the ingredients well. 7. Add beaten eggs into the mixture. 8. Pour into a wok and spread evenly. 9. Take a small bowl and add the sugar and the butter. 10. Mix them until the mixture becomes smooth. 11. Add the salt as required. 12. Simmer it for about twenty-five minutes. 13. Your dish is ready to be served with crushed peanuts and walnuts. 14. You can refrigerate your dessert as well.

Delicious Cornstarch with Berries and Pork Balls

Prep Time: 10 minutes | Cook Time: 35 minutes | Serves: 4

½ cup sticky rice
1 egg
1 (1 inch) piece ginger root, minced
2 teaspoons soy sauce
Salt, to taste
4 ounces (113 g) ground pork
2 tablespoons cornstarch
1 tablespoon pork stock
¼ cup water
1 teaspoon dried goji berries

1. Soak the rice in the water for 2 hours in a bowl. 2. Mix the pork stock, pork, water, salt, soy sauce, ginger, cornstarch, and goji berries in a bowl. 3. Divide the mixture into meatballs. 4. Fill a cooking pot with the water and set a steamer basket inside. 5. Boil the water and spread the balls in the basket. 6. Cover and steam these balls for 30 minutes. 7. Coat these steamed balls with the rice. 8. Sear the steamed balls in a Mandarin wok greased with the oil for 5 minutes. 9. Serve warm.

Crispy Oniony Coconut Shrimp

Prep Time: 15 minutes | Cook Time: 5 minutes | Serves: 4

1 pound (454 g) shrimp
¼ cup all-purpose flour
1 teaspoon cornstarch
¼ teaspoon baking powder
¼ teaspoon baking soda
¼ teaspoon salt
¼ teaspoon garlic powder
¼ teaspoon onion powder
¼ cup ice water
½ cup coconut flakes
Peanut oil, for frying

1. Whisk the flour, cornstarch, baking soda, salt, garlic powder, baking powder, and onion powder in a bowl. 2. Dredge the shrimp through the flour mixture then dip in the water. 3. Coat the shrimp with the coconut flakes. 4. Deep the fry the shrimp in a Cantonese wok filled with oil at 350ºF (180ºC), until golden-brown. 5. Transfer these shrimps to a plate lined with a paper towel. 6. Serve warm.

Homemade Fried Sesame with Sugar Balls

Prep Time: 15 minutes | Cook Time: 5 minutes | Serves: 4

1½ cups glutinous rice flour
1/3 cup granulated sugar
¼ cup boiling water
¼ cup water
7 ounces (198 g) lotus paste or red bean paste
¼ cup sesame seeds
4 cups peanut oil, for frying

1. Mix the sugar, ¼ cup rice flour, and ¼ cup warm water in a bowl and leave for 5 minutes. 2. Stir in the remaining water, and remaining rice flour. 3. Mix well, cover the dough, and leave it for 30 minutes. 4. Meanwhile, make 8 small balls out of the lotus paste. 5. Divide the prepared dough into 8 pieces and spread each piece of dough into a round. 6. Place one lotus paste ball at the center of each dough round and wrap it around the ball. 7. Roll to smooth out the balls then coat them with sesame seeds. 8. Add 4 cups oil in a deep wok and heat it to 320ºF (160ºC). 9. Deep fry the sesame balls until golden-brown. 10. Serve.

Spicy Pork and Cabbage Potstickers

Prep Time: 15 minutes | Cook Time: 3 minutes | Serves: 6

½ pound (227g) ground pork
1 cup finely shredded cabbage
2 scallions, sliced
2 teaspoons minced ginger
2 tablespoons soy sauce
1 teaspoon sesame oil
½ teaspoon pepper
24 dumpling skins
2 tablespoons vegetable oil
¼ cup water
¼ cup chopped scallions

1. In a large bowl, combine the pork, cabbage, scallions, ginger, soy sauce, sesame oil, and pepper. Refrigerate for 30 minutes. 2. Take 1 dumpling skin and use your finger to brush water along the edge of the circle. Place about 1 tablespoon of the mixture in the center of the skin. Fold the dumpling skin over and firmly press the sides to seal completely. While you are forming the potstickers, create a flattened bottom. You can also pleat the edges if you like. 3. Heat the oil in a wok over medium heat. Place the potstickers, flattened side down, in one layer and fry for 1 to 2 minutes. 4. Carefully pour the water into the wok and cover. Allow the pot stickers to steam for an additional 2 to 3 minutes. Remove the lid and cook until the water has evaporated. 5. Place the potstickers on a plate and sprinkle the tops with the scallions. Serve hot.

Crispy Fried Shrimp Balls

Prep Time: 10 minutes | Cook Time: 5 minutes | Serves: 16

1 pound (454 g) shelled and deveined shrimp
1 egg white, lightly beaten
1 teaspoon salt
1 teaspoon sugar
1 tablespoon cornstarch
½ teaspoon sesame oil
3 dashes white pepper powder
8 pieces spring roll wrapper

1. Blend the shrimp with the egg white, salt, cornstarch, sugar, sesame oil, and white pepper in a bowl. 2. Cut the roll wrappers into strips and keep them in a bowl. 3. Make the small meatballs out of the shrimp mixture and wrap them with the roll wrapper strips. 4. Heat oil in a Cantonese wok and deep fry the shrimp ball until golden-brown. 5. Serve warm.

Yummy Milky Coconut and Peanut Mochi

Prep Time: 10 minutes | Cook Time: 18 minutes | Serves: 14

For the Dough:
1½ cups sweet rice flour
¼ cup cornstarch
¼ cup caster sugar
1½ cups coconut milk
2 tablespoons coconut oil

For the Filling:
½ cup peanuts
½ cup coconut flakes, chopped
3 tablespoons sugar
1 tablespoon melted coconut oil

For the Coconut Peanut Mochi:
A large piece of wax paper
1 cup coconut flakes, chopped
16 small paper cupcake cups

1. Add the peanuts to a Mandarin wok and roast them for 3 to 5 minutes until golden-brown. 2. Allow the peanuts to cool, then chop them finely. 3. Layer a 11-inch by 11-inch cake pan with the wax paper and brush with vegetable oil. 4. Whisk the rice flour, sugar, cornstarch, coconut oil, and coconut milk in a bowl. 5. Boil the water in a suitable cooking pot, place the steam rack inside and add the dough in the steamer. 6. Cover and cook for 15 minutes in the steamer then allow the dough to cool. 7. Meanwhile, mix the peanuts with 1 tablespoon coconut oil, sugar, and coconut flakes in a bowl. 8. Spread the prepared dough in the prepared pan and cut it into 14 squares. 9. Add a tablespoon the filling at the center of each square. 10. Pinch the edges of each square and roll it into a ball. 11. Coat all the balls with the coconut flakes and place them in the cupcake cup. 12. Leave them for 20 minutes. Serve.

Healthy Chili Cilantro and Seaweed Salad

Prep Time: 15 minutes | Cook Time: 16 minutes | Serves: 12

12 ounces (340 g) fresh kelp
4 garlic cloves, minced
3 thin ginger slices, minced
3 Thai chilies, sliced
2 scallions, chopped
3 tablespoons vegetable oil
1 tablespoon Sichuan peppercorns
1½ teaspoons sugar
2 teaspoons Chinese black vinegar
2½ tablespoons light soy sauce
1 teaspoon oyster sauce
½ to 1 teaspoon sesame oil, to taste
¼ teaspoon salt
¼ teaspoon five-spice powder
1 tablespoon cilantro, chopped

1. Boil the kelp in a pot filled with water for 5 minutes in a cooking pot. 2. Drain the kelp and rinse it under cold water. 3. Mix the ginger, garlic, Thai chilies, and scallion in a bowl. 4. Sauté the garlic mixture, and peppercorns with 3 tablespoons oil in a Mandarin wok for 10 minutes. 5. Stir in the vinegar, sugar, soy sauce, salt, sesame oil, five-spice powder, and oyster oil. 6. Add cilantro and scallions then sauté for 1 minute. 7. Pour this sauce over the boiled kelp leaves. 8. Serve warm.

Healthy Sugar and Vinegar with Cucumber Salad

Prep Time: 10 minutes | Cook Time: 2 minutes | Serves: 4

6 garlic cloves, minced
3 tablespoons oil
2 English cucumbers, sliced
1½ teaspoon salt
1 teaspoon sugar
⅛ teaspoon MSG
¼ teaspoon sesame oil
1 tablespoon rice vinegar

1. Sauté the garlic with oil in a Cantonese wok for 30 seconds. 2. Stir in the sugar, MSG, sesame oil, rice vinegar, and salt. 3. Cook for 1 minute, then toss in cucumber. 4. Mix well and serve.

Ketchup Cucumber with Koya Dofu

Prep Time: 10 minutes | Cook Time: 7 minutes | Serves: 6

1 Koya dofu, sliced
1 katakuriko
2 tablespoons vegetable oil
3 tablespoons ketchup
1 tablespoon soy sauce
2 teaspoons sugar
1 cucumber, peeled and sliced

1. Squeeze the dofu and slice it. 2. Coat the dofu slices with Katakuriko. 3. Mix the ketchup, soy sauce, and sugar in a bowl. 4. Add oil to a wok and sear the dofu for 4 to 5 minutes per side. 5. Stir in the prepared sauce and cook it for 3 minutes on a simmer. 6. Garnish with the cucumber. 7. Serve warm.

Peppered Sesame Edamame

Prep Time: 5 minutes | Cook Time: 5 minutes | Serves: 4

1 (16 ounces/454 g) package frozen edamame
2 teaspoons sesame seeds
3 tablespoons white sugar
2 tablespoons soy sauce
2 teaspoons olive oil
1 teaspoon red pepper flakes

1. Fill a cooking pot with the boiling water and soak the edamame in the water for 6 minutes. 2. Transfer the edamame to a salad bowl. 3. Sauté edamame with olive oil in a Mandarin wok for 5 minutes. 4. Stir in the sugar, sesame seeds, soy sauce, and red pepper flakes. 5. Mix well and serve.

Refreshing Lime Parsley Calamari

Prep Time: 10 minutes | Cook Time: 2 minutes | Serves: 4

½ cup Tequila Lime Marinade
1 pound (454 g) calamari tubes, cut into 1″ pieces
2 tablespoons vegetable oil
1 tablespoon lime juice
2 tablespoons extra-virgin olive oil
2 tablespoons chopped Italian parsley
½ teaspoon kosher salt

1. Combine the marinade with the calamari in a large bowl. Refrigerate for 5 minutes. 2. Heat a wok to medium-high heat and add the vegetable oil. Swirl the oil around the wok and add the calamari. Toss and stir-fry the calamari for 2 to 3 minutes. 3. Remove the calamari to a plate and drizzle with the lime juice, olive oil, and parsley. Season with the salt and serve immediately.

Nutritious Carrots and Scallion Egg Rolls

Prep Time: 15 minutes | Cook Time: 5 minutes | Serves: 12

1 pound (454 g) lean ground pork
1 tablespoon dark soy sauce
2 tablespoons oyster sauce
1 teaspoon minced garlic, divided
1 teaspoon minced ginger, divided
1 cup shredded carrots
2 scallions, finely chopped
1 teaspoon sesame oil
1 teaspoon black pepper
25 (6 × 6) egg roll wrappers
2 eggs, beaten
2 cups peanut or vegetable oil

1. In a large bowl, mix together the ground pork, soy sauce, oyster sauce, garlic, ginger, carrots, scallions, and sesame oil. Add the black pepper. 2. One at a time, place an eggroll wrapper on a flat surface with one of the points facing toward you. Spoon about 2 tablespoons of the filling in a line toward the bottom half of the wrapper. Brush the top corner and sides with the beaten egg. Fold in the sides of the wrapper and tightly roll the egg roll up until it is closed. Press to seal, set aside, and continue with the remaining ingredients. 3. Heat the oil in a wok over high heat to 375°F (190°C). Working in batches, fry the egg rolls until golden brown, about 5 to 6 minutes. Remove the fried egg rolls to plates lined with paper towels to drain. Serve hot.

Minty Lettuce Spring Rolls

Prep Time: 15 minutes | Cook Time: 2 minutes | Serves: 4

½ pound (227g) shrimp, peeled and deveined
2 garlic cloves, minced
2 tablespoons fish sauce
¼ teaspoon black pepper
2 tablespoons vegetable oil
8 rice paper spring roll wrappers
8 lettuce leaves
2 cups cooked vermicelli noodles
1 cup cucumbers, thinly sliced
1 cup shredded carrots
1 cup fresh mint leaves
1 cup cilantro leaves
1½ cups Nuoc Cham Sauce

1. Mix the shrimp, garlic, fish sauce, and black pepper together in a medium bowl. Refrigerate for 10 minutes. 2. Heat a wok with the oil over medium-high heat. Place in the shrimp and stir-fry for 2 to 3 minutes, until they turn pink. Remove to a plate. 3. Take 1 piece of rice paper and dip into a shallow dish of water to soften. Lay the softened rice paper on a plate. Place 1 piece of lettuce in the center and top with ¼ cup of the noodles in a line. Top with a few cooked shrimps, slices of cucumber, carrots, mint leaves, and cilantro. Fold in the sides and tightly roll up until it is closed. Repeat with the remaining ingredients. 4. Serve with Nuoc Cham Sauce.

Nutritious Eggy Crab Lettuce Warps

Prep Time: 10 minutes | Cook Time: 10 minutes | Serves: 4-6

1 head lettuce
4 eggs, lightly beaten
Pinch salt to taste
Pinch ground white pepper to taste
½ teaspoon soy sauce
2 scallions, chopped
3 tablespoons peanut oil
½ cup diced water chestnuts
1 small onion, thinly sliced
¾ cup crabmeat
¼ cup Basic Sambal (here) (optional)

1. Wash and separate the lettuce leaves. Chill the lettuce leaves in the refrigerator until just before serving. 2. Put the beaten eggs into a medium bowl. Add the salt, pepper, soy sauce, and scallions to the eggs. Stir gently just to combine. 3. In a wok over medium-high heat, heat the peanut oil. 4. Stir-fry the water chestnuts and onion until the onion is slightly translucent. 5. Add the crabmeat to the wok, then the egg mixture, and let it sit for a moment. When the bottom of the egg is cooked through, flip, and cook on the other side. 6. Using a wok spatula, break up and scramble the egg. 7. Serve with the chilled lettuce leaves and sambal (if using).

Conclusion

There you have it!

Chinese food is famous and contains all the nutrients that metabolism and body require to remain healthy. Now you are armed with all of the best tasting Chinese recipes that you will need. Remember, to become a master at making all of the latest Chinese food recipes; you have to understand the basics of Chinese cuisine. The basic techniques of Chinese food are frying, deep-frying, steaming, boiling, and roasting. The more you practice, the better you will become at making these delicious recipes.

With that being said, I highly recommend that you try making all of the recipes listed in this book at least once. Good luck, and always remember, have fun while you are making these dishes.

Happy cooking!

Appendix 1 Measurement Conversion Chart

VOLUME EQUIVALENTS (LIQUID)

US STANDARD	US STANDARD (OUNCES)	METRIC (APPROXIMATE)
2 tablespoons	1 fl.oz	30 mL
¼ cup	2 fl.oz	60 mL
½ cup	4 fl.oz	120 mL
1 cup	8 fl.oz	240 mL
1½ cup	12 fl.oz	355 mL
2 cups or 1 pint	16 fl.oz	475 mL
4 cups or 1 quart	32 fl.oz	1 L
1 gallon	128 fl.oz	4 L

TEMPERATURES EQUIVALENTS

FAHRENHEIT (F)	CELSIUS (C) (APPROXIMATE)
225 °F	107 °C
250 °F	120 °C
275 °F	135 °C
300 °F	150 °C
325 °F	160 °C
350 °F	180 °C
375 °F	190 °C
400 °F	205 °C
425 °F	220 °C
450 °F	235 °C
475 °F	245 °C
500 °F	260 °C

VOLUME EQUIVALENTS (DRY)

US STANDARD	METRIC (APPROXIMATE)
⅛ teaspoon	0.5 mL
¼ teaspoon	1 mL
½ teaspoon	2 mL
¾ teaspoon	4 mL
1 teaspoon	5 mL
1 tablespoon	15 mL
¼ cup	59 mL
½ cup	118 mL
¾ cup	177 mL
1 cup	235 mL
2 cups	475 mL
3 cups	700 mL
4 cups	1 L

WEIGHT EQUIVALENTS

US STANDARD	METRIC (APPROXINATE)
1 ounce	28 g
2 ounces	57 g
5 ounces	142 g
10 ounces	284 g
15 ounces	425 g
16 ounces (1 pound)	455 g
1.5pounds	680 g
2pounds	907 g

Appendix 2 Recipes Index

Made in the USA
Coppell, TX
20 September 2024